The Kelsey Papers

The Kelsey Papers

With an Introduction by
John Warkentin (York University)

and including the Introduction to the 1929 edition by
Arthur G. Doughty (Keeper of Public Records)
and Chester Martin (Head of the Department of History, University of Manitoba)

Canadian Plains Research Center
University of Regina
1994

Canadian Plains Research Center
University of Regina
Regina, Saskatchewan S4S 0A2
Canada

Canadian Cataloguing in Publication Data
Kelsey, Henry, ca. 1670-ca. 1724
The Kelsey papers
(Canadian plains studies, ISSN 0317-6290 ; 29)
Includes bibliographical references.
ISBN 0-88977-085-9

1. Kelsey, Henry, ca. 1670-ca. 1724 - Diaries
2. Kelsey, Henry, ca. 1670-ca. 1724 - Journeys -
Prairie Provinces. 3. Explorers - Prairie Provinces -
Diaries. 4. Explorers - England - Diaries.
5. Northwest, Canadian - Discovery and exploration,
English. I. Warkentin, John, 1928-
II. Doughty, Arthur G. (Arthur George), Sir, 1860-1936.
III. Martin, Chester, 1882-1958. IV. University of
Regina. Canadian Plains Research Center. V. Title.
VI. Series

FC3211.1.K44A3 1994 971.24'01 C94-920280
F1060.7.K32A 1994

Cover Design: Agnes Bray/Brian Mlazgar
Cover photo courtesy of Courtney Milne

Printed and bound in Canada by
Hignell Printing Limited, Winnipeg, Manitoba
Printed on acid-free paper

CONTENTS

Publisher's Preface vi
Introduction to the 1994 Edition vii
1. Journey to the Plains: The First Year, 1690 xiii
2. Journey to the Plains: The Second Year, 1691 xiv
3. Beliefs and Customs of the Plains Indians xvii
4. Journey into the Barren Grounds, 1689 xviii
5. Letter to Mr. Smith, 1694 xix
6. Passage from England to the Vicinity of Cape Farewell, 1696 xix
7. Daily Life at York Fort, 1694 xx
8. Daily Life at York Fort, 1696 to 1697 xxi
9. Passage from England to James Bay, 1698 xxiv
10. Letter Dated Albany Fort, 5 September 1701 xxiv
11. Kelsey's Summary of His Activities for the Hudson's Bay Company, 1684 to 1722 xxiv
Bibliography xxv
Introduction to the 1929 Edition xxvii
(a) The Kelsey Papers xxvii
(b) The Kelsey Tradition xxviii
(c) Kelsey's Own Story xxxi
(d) Kelsey and the Company xxxv
(e) Kelsey's Route in 1691 xl
Notes xliii
Facsimile of Page of Original Manuscript, in Kelsey's Handwriting xlvii
The Kelsey Papers 1
Kelsey's Introduction to the *Journal* of 1690 1
The *Journal* of 1691 3
Indian "Belief and Superstitions" 11
The Churchill *Journal*, June 17-August 8, 1689 15
Kelsey to Smith, August 8, 1694 20
Journal, Hudson's Bay frigate, June 2-July 19, 1696 20
Journal, York Fort, August 13-October 4, 1694 24
Journal, York Fort, September 18, 1696-September 3, 1697 29
Journal, *Deering* frigate, June 13-August 15, 1698 75
Kelsey to the Hudson's Bay Company, September 5, 1701 78
Kelsey's *Memorandum*, 1683-1722 79
Index 83
Map .... end of volume

PUBLISHERS PREFACE

Sixty-five years have elapsed since the Public Archives of Canada and the Public Record Office of Northern Ireland first published Henry Kelsey's papers, namely, his journals, letters and memoranda dealing with his long career as a servant with the Hudson's Bay Company from 1684 to 1722.

The papers, long forgotten, came to public attention in 1926, when they were discovered among documents presented to the Public Record Office of Northern Ireland by Major A. F. Dobbs, of Castle Dobbs, Carrickfergus. How they came into the possession of Major Dobbs remains a mystery.

It is a sad reflection on our indifference to history that the papers have remained out of print these many years. They offer the first written description and impression of two vast regions of North America where humans ventured forth at great risk: the Barrens of the North and thc Prairies of the interior.

More important, they provide a remarkable record of the ingenuity of those people who first adapted to the Barrens and the Prairies and called them home; the same peoples who the Europeans became dependent upon for survival; the same peoples they chose to describe as "savages."

In reprinting the original 1929 edition of Kelsey's papers, the Canadian Plains Research Center is grateful to Professor John Warkentin of the Department of Geography, York University, for setting the papers in context and providing the reader with an appropriate new Introduction to Kelsey's documents. The Canadian Plains Research Center also wishes to express its gratitude to the copyright holder of the 1929 edition, the Deputy Keeper of the Records, Public Record Office of Northern Ireland, who graciously granted permission to reprint the Kelsey Papers. Those interested in examining the original manuscript may contact the Public Record Office of Northern Ireland, 66 Balmoral Avenue, Belfast BT9 6NY (reference D.162/7).

The 1929 publications contains an excellent translation into French of the original Introduction by Arthur G. Doughty and Chester Martin. The translation was not included in this publication for reasons of economy.

James N. McCrorie
Executive Director
Canadian Plains Research Center
November 1994

INTRODUCTION TO THE 1994 EDITION

John Warkentin

Henry Kelsey, a late-seventeenth-century Englishman who spent most of his life as a fur trader on Hudson Bay, is best known for his journey in 1690-92 from the Bay to the great interior plains of present-day Canada. And rightly so, since he has the distinction of being the first European to see and describe part of the Canadian Plains and the Native people who lived there. But his association with Canada was much longer and deeper than that two-year journey. Even before the inland trip he had walked a considerable distance along the coast of Hudson Bay, north of Churchill, another first for a European. But these two journeys are just brief highlights in a long career as a Hudson's Bay Company (HBC) servant and officer stationed on the Bay from 1684 to 1722, a span of thirty-eight years with only short breaks back in England.

From Kelsey's journals reprinted in this publication we learn of his two land/canoe journeys, about voyaging from England to northern North America, about life at York Factory on the shore of Hudson Bay, and of the warfare between the English and French in that region.

Looking at a map of Canada, many persons at first glance see a great mediterranean sea, Hudson Bay, which surely must be a centre of transportation activity in the country. When the "On to the Bay" railway was being finished in the 1920s such rosy views were still in the air, but climate and ice have precluded great development. Hudson Bay, the centerpiece of this interior North American geography, is ice-covered most of the year. By July most of the ice is gone, but freeze-up begins in September. Along the shore the ice is continuous in winter, tight to the land; in the middle of the Bay there are ice floes usually in constant motion, though this was only known once there were regular aerial reconnaissance surveys. Yet the HBC for generations used the Bay as its base of Canadian operations, and Kelsey was in the vanguard in leading the Company's servants inland into new environments.

About one-half of the land area of Canada is forested, and the southern shore of Hudson Bay is roughly the boundary between forest and tundra, one of the great transition zones in Canada. This is commonly known as the tree line. Only two great extensive treeless areas exist in Canada: the prairies of the interior Plains, and the Barren Lands north of the tree line. These regions, both reconnoitered and reported on by Kelsey, have remained highly distinctive within Canada, though of course with wrenching human changes. The grasslands were transformed by the largest human migrations this country has ever seen and were turned into an agricultural community in the nineteenth and early twentieth centuries. Life too has changed drastically in the Barren Grounds, because after the 1950s the Inuit came "in from the land" and under government urging and assistance were resettled in villages some of which were placed along the very coast Kelsey traversed in the late 1680s.

What are the great geographical regions like in which Kelsey lived and which he visited? Hudson Bay occupies a depressed part of the Canadian Shield, and along its southern margins are the low, exceedingly flat, poorly drained, sedimentary beds of the Hudson Bay lowland. South of York Fort you quickly leave the lowland and enter the glaciated Canadian Shield: bare, rugged igneous and metamorphic rock knobs, rapids-strewn streams, countless lakes, boreal forest, and limited parent material for soil. Along the southwestern margins of the Shield there is poorly drained morainic hill and pond country, still closely forested, and with deep accumulations of loose weathered parent materials, the beginnings of a foundation for soils. The bedrock, overlapping the Shield and extending far to the west and south, is sedimentary again, similar to that of the Hudson Bay lowland; these are the immense plains. Away from the Shield the land is higher, mostly well drained, and the climate warmer and drier. Palliser's map of 1865 vividly shows and describes the landscapes to come as we continue southward into the plains. First there is a mix of meadows and clumps of wood, fittingly called a park country by the fur traders who came after Kelsey and compared this landscape to the parks of English estates. Then dramatically one is in the open grassland plains, stretching endlessly, yet far more varied than they often are alleged to be. Much of this topography is undulating ground moraine, crossed by great rivers flowing in impressive valleys. There are many low tablelands or hills, commonly covered by rough, hummocky moraines with their many ponds, and locally wooded.

All these lands from Hudson Bay to the plains had long been settled by Natives, by Algonquian-speaking Woodland Cree near York Fort and in the Shield, and by Plains Cree and Siouan-speaking Assiniboine in the grasslands. There were other communities on the plains, such as the Algonquian-speaking Blackfoot and Atsina Gros Ventres, and the Siouan-speaking Hidatsa, associated with the Mandan Indians, all dependent to a great extent on buffalo. In the time of Kelsey, a few decades before the arrival of horses, life was a constant round of movement, on foot and, where possible, by canoe.

To the north of Churchill the Shield extends all the way to the Arctic Ocean, not a high land but an extremely rough country, with much stony glacial debris and turbulent streams which have barely cut valleys into the surface. The tree line approximately follows the south coast of Hudson Bay and then angles northwestward toward the mouth of the Mackenzie River, a line partly corresponding to the boundary of the proposed new administrative territory of Nunavut. Modern official tourist maps of the Northwest Territories mark the tree line, demonstrating its importance in the life of this land. Beyond the tree line the tundra area became generally known to fur traders as the Barren Grounds, a term still widely used. Great herds of caribou migrated seasonally across this region, and until the latter part of the nineteenth century musk oxen lived there too. Inuit lived along the coast, dependent upon seals; they also moved inland to hunt caribou and musk oxen. To the west and northwest were the Athapaskan-speaking Chipewyan, the Dene, often called the Northern Indians by fur traders. This was a thinly populated land, with frequent movement from one area to another, an essential element in the life of the inhabitants.

Kelsey on his journey to the plains, lists six Native groups in his journals. The Nayhaythaway are the Cree. The Home Indians, also known as the Home Guard, are the Indians close to York Fort who provided the fort with food by hunting; they, too, are mainly Cree. The Stone Indians with whom Kelsey did most of his travelling are the Assiniboine. The Eagles brich Indians cannot be identified, but are likely a small local plains group who were living in what is present-day east/central Saskatchewan when the Indians Kelsey was travelling with encountered them. The Mountain Poets are another plains group which also cannot be identified. Probably they are a Siouan-speaking Assiniboine band living in the vicinity of the Manitoba Escarpment. The eastward-facing front of the escarpment is divided into broad segments called hills and mountains, for example the Porcupine Hills, and the Duck and Riding Mountains. The term "poet" has been frequently discussed in the literature on Kelsey, and is thought to be his rendering of "pwat," the Cree word for the Sioux. To identify the Naywatame Poets is the most intriguing problem of all because those Indians were the goal of Kelsey's travels. Many scholars have examined the perplexing question of who they were, but the group's identity remains conjectural. Suggestions have ranged from the Blackfoot to the Atsina Gros Ventres. Dale Russell, who has analyzed the meaning of the word Naywatame, has suggested that they are a group of Hidatsa. The Hidatsa were centred in what is present-day North Dakota, but in Kelsey's time they may have travelled seasonally northward into what is present-day Saskatchewan. Russell's careful interpretation is based on the meaning of "wate," a hole, cave, or den, and he argues that it may refer to the Hidatsa's partly subterranean earthern dwellings, similar to those of the Mandans. (Russell, 1993: 82-85)

After the journey to the plains, when he was stationed at York Fort, Kelsey also mentions a few of the groups referred to above, including the Stone Indians, when they came to the fort to trade. He refers to "plains Indians," likely a general term for the Indians of the interior. The Indians who live close to the fort (the Home Guard Cree) are mentioned constantly and there is a reference to an "upland Indian," presumably from a place farther away than where the Home Indians lived. As well there are references to Mohawks, first mainly in connection with the French during their occupation of part of Hudson Bay, though some also stayed on in the area when the English controlled York Fort. On his northern land exploration there are references to the "northern Indians" and the "dog-side" nation, that is, the Chipewyan and the Dogrib Indians, and by way of contrast he refers to the "southern Indians" (that is, all the others). He also mentions the Eskimoes (the Inuit) of the west coast of Hudson Bay.

These then were the lands and some of the peoples where Kelsey spent most of his life after he arrived in Hudson Bay in 1684 as a youth of about 17, and until two years before he died in England in 1724 in his 57th(?) year. Little is known of Kelsey's origins. Even the year of his birth, thought to be 1667, is not certain. He was apprenticed to the HBC in 1684, and came to York Fort that year. He spent his career with the Company, rising in 1718 to be governor of York Fort and all the HBC's establishments on Hudson Bay, a position he held until his retirement in 1722.

After living only a few years on the Bay, Kelsey's energy and willingness, his ability to walk long distances across difficult terrain, and his skill in hunting and living off the land clearly were known to his superiors. Already in 1688/89 he had undertaken, with one Indian companion, to carry a winter packet eastward from York Fort to New Severn along the coast of Hudson Bay, a task three Indians had failed at. The next summer he was sent northward on his journey into the Barren Grounds, and then when he was 23 he was despatched southward on his great two-year journey into the interior of the continent. This was a time when it was difficult to get any HBC servants to travel inland from the Bayside posts. Kelsey's journeys were undertaken either with an Indian companion or with Indian communities. He was known for his friendly relationships with Indians, and was also deeply concerned that cordial relations be maintained between HBC men and Native peoples. When he was governor Kelsey even reprimanded a senior officer when he did not conform. As a fur trader, Kelsey's daily life was inevitably and intimately linked to the Native inhabitants. In no way could European fur traders survive at posts in the nonagricultural parts of North America or travel into the interior, without the assistance of Natives in trapping fur-bearing animals, trading pelts, teaching the craft of travelling within a northern wilderness, and taking travellers with them in their community movements or trading journeys. What is particularly impressive is the annual journey which Plains Indians made across the Shield from the interior to the Bay, a journey made by very few southern Canadians today, even by rail or air.

Kelsey was adept at languages. He knew Cree, Assiniboine, and perhaps had some knowledge of other Native languages, a rare accomplishment amongst HBC men of his generation. He taught his fellow servants Native words, and even prepared a Cree vocabulary printed by the Company. A copy of this long-lost pamphlet of seven folio pages, titled *A Dictionary of the Hudson' Bay Indian Language,* but with no author named on the title page, was identified in the 1970s in the collections of the British Library, London, by H.C. Wolfart and D.H. Pentland (Wolfart and Pentland, 1979).

Kelsey's years of service for the HBC largely overlapped the battles between the English and the French for control of Hudson Bay, a conflict that was not resolved in favour of the English in these territories until the Treaty of Utrecht of 1713. In the course of his career Kelsey was stationed at various times at York Fort, but during the long period the French held that post, from 1697 to 1714, he was at other posts on James Bay which still were controlled by the Company. When the French held York Fort they called it Fort Bourbon. In his later years on James Bay Kelsey was deputy governor at Albany, and chief at Eastmain. Kelsey had leave back in England in 1703-05 and 1712-14.

The yearly fur trade routine and partcular responsibilities of the HBC servants were well established at the posts, but there was considerable variety in Kelsey's life. As well as a fur trader, he was a seaman who had acquired navigational skills, and he served as the mate of the ship on one of his voyages out from England, and he may have served as navigation officer on another voyage. On James Bay he was master of a ship sailing out of Albany Fort, conducting the fur trade at Eastmain, on the east side of James Bay. Navigation was hazardous on both Hudson and James Bays, especially along the Hudson Bay lowland shore. Shallow water, shoals, storms, and considerable tidal ranges caused problems for shipping, and Kelsey was all too often involved in piloting ships in savage waters, assisting grounded vessels after marine mishaps, and salvaging cargoes.

Although no further great journeys were demanded of Kelsey as he settled into a long career with the HBC and the life of a trader at the Bay, the energetic travelling and enthusiastic outdoor life which marked his early years remained with him. He seems to have taken every opportunity to be away from whatever post he was stationed at — heading for a nearby marsh, coast, river, or forest, usually doing outdoor chores or hunting caribou, deer, geese, and other wildlife, trying to bring country food to the forts. He likely was one of the HBC's leaders, at the very least by his example, in trying to make the posts less dependent on provisions from England.

Profound and unwelcome breaks to the normal life of the posts resulted from the conflict between the English and the French. Kelsey was present at two of the successful French attacks on York Fort in 1694 and 1697, and, indeed, on both occasions was one of the HBC governor's emissaries in arranging to surrender. In each instance he was taken as prisoner to France, released there, returned to England, rejoined the service of the HBC, and went back to the Bay. Including his return trips on leave to England after completing a term of service, and the forced crossings with the French, he made a total of twelve voyages across the Atlantic over the period from 1684 to 1722. His attraction to the activities of a fur trade post on an inland sea, his fondness for wilderness life, and his congenial associations with Native people must have drawn him back time and again to the service of the HBC and to the Bay.

In 1714, on the return of York Fort to the HBC by the Treaty of Utrecht, James Knight was made governor of York Fort and all the Company's posts on Hudson and James Bays, and Kelsey was made deputy governor. On Knight's retirement in 1718 Kelsey became governor. Like so many HBC men in the seventeenth and eighteenth centuries, they were both aware of the stories told by the northern Indians of far-off copper and gold mines in distant northern parts of the Barren Grounds. Knight became obsessed with finding a way to the alleged gold mines by the North-West Passage, and after he retired he led an exploring expedition in 1719 to northwestern Hudson Bay. This expedition of two ships sailing from England was sponsored by the HBC, always interested in commercial gain. Kelsey, now governor, was also interested in exploring northward from York Fort and Churchill, in his case searching for the more plausible copper deposits and hoping to expand trade. During his years as governor he ordered summer explorations northward by ship, and he himself sailed north in 1719 and 1721, with no success in finding minerals, but the voyages succeeded in establishing better relations with the Inuit. The governing committee of the HBC in London disapproved his ambitious plan of 1721 to winter at Churchill in order to carry out his proposed explorations more effectively. Whatever his position in the HBC, there is consistency in Kelsey during his years of service in North America. We can see the same energy and curiosity in acquiring greater knowledge and understanding of new lands and peoples in Kelsey the mature governor that was present in Kelsey the young explorer.

After Kelsey retired to England in 1722, he applied to the HBC to captain one of their ships to Hudson Bay in 1724, but the vessel he had petitioned for did not sail that year, and his service to the Company was finally ended. He had married an East Greenwich woman in England in 1698, after his second return from France, and they had three children. In England, Kelsey lived in East Greenwich, where he owned a house. He died there in the fall of 1724.

An important objective in making Kelsey's journals available again is that it is hoped that the rich material they contain will stimulate further study of late-seventeenth and early-eighteenth-century life on Hudson Bay and in interior North

America, including the life and role of Kelsey himself. A great deal more needs to be done in elucidating and interpreting Kelsey's journals, and placing them in the context of North American history, geography and literature.

*****

The papers printed here consist of accounts by Kelsey of six significant episodes in his career, including his two exploratory journeys, and also of short letters and a memorandum. They may have been copies for his own use of journals he had prepared for the Hudson's Bay Company, since lost. It is not certain that the manuscript is in Kelsey's handwriting, except, it appears for some words written in Cree. It consists of a bound volume of 128 pages which was given in 1926 to the Public Record Office of Northern Ireland by Major A.F. Dobbs of Castle Dobbs, Carrickfergus, Northern Ireland. It had been part of the library of Arthur Dobbs, a strong and frequent critic of the Hudson's Bay Company in the eighteenth century. How Dobbs got the manuscripts is not known. It was published in 1929 as a joint publication of the Public Archives of Canada and the Public Record Office of Northern Ireland, as The Kelsey Papers, with an introduction by A.G. Doughty and Chester Martin. (The present publication is based on that edition.) James F. Kenney of the Public Archives of Canada staff must be credited for overseeing the careful transcription of the manuscript, and also for assiduously searching through contemporary HBC and other records for information on Kelsey's life for a fine essay "The Career of Henry Kelsey," published in 1929 in the Transactions of the Royal Society of Canada.

Two slightly variant accounts of Kelsey's 1791 travels in the plains were printed in the British Parliamentary Papers in 1749, as part of the Hudson's Bay Company's evidence before the government's inquiry into the operations of the Company. Those accounts are very similar to that reproduced here, and were likely submitted to support the Company's contention that it indeed had endeavoured to explore and develop the hinterland behind Hudson Bay, as it was expected to do. Word of mouth stories had also been passed along that there had been an inland journey by a Company servant named Henry Kelsey. Since the account in the Parliamentary Papers included no background on the journey or on Kelsey, critics of the Company, such as Joseph Robson, who maintained that the HBC had not fulfilled the obligations in its charter to advance trade and development, cast doubt on whether the Company had actually sent Kelsey on his journey, suggesting, indeed, that after differences with the Bayside governor of the HBC he had gone on his own with the Plains Indians into the interior (Robson, 1752: 72-74). The great contribution of Kelsey's manuscript was that it not only confirmed his travels, but added much new detail on his activities, established that the HBC had sent Kelsey to the interior, corrected misrepresentations, and revived interest in this important explorer of our country.

*****

Three main kinds of activities involving Kelsey's services for the Hudson's Bay Company are included in the journals: Kelsey's accounts of his two explorations, logs of two of his voyages from England across the Atlantic, and daily entries from two of his York Fort journals. In addition there is a description of the life of the Plains Indians, two letters, and a memorandum outlining his career. All this material is arranged in a deliberate order. The journeys to the plains and the

Barren Grounds come first, with the vital plains journey placed right at the beginning, even though it occurred two years after the northward trip.

The journals are arranged in the following order. The number of pages in the manuscript are given in square brackets.

1. Description in verse of the journey from York Fort to the plains and travels on the plains, 12 June 1690 to September/October (?) 1690. [3 pages]
2. Journal of the travels on the plains, 15 July 1691 to 12 September 1691, in search of the Naywatame Poets. [11 pages]
3. Descriptions of the customs, beliefs and superstitions of the Plains Indians as observed in 1690-91. [5 pages]
4. Journal of the journey north of Churchill River into the Barren Grounds, 17 June 1689 to 8 August 1689. [5 pages]
5. Letter from Kelsey to Mr. Smith, dated York Fort, 8 August 1694. [1 page]
6. Log of ocean voyage from Gravesend, England, to off Cape Farewell, Greenland, enroute to Hudson Bay, 2 June 1696 to 19 July 1696. [5 pages]
7. Daily journal kept at York Fort, 13 August 1694 to 4 October 1694. [6 pages]
8. Daily journal kept at York Fort, 18 September 1696 to 3 September 1697. [81 pages]
9. Log of ocean voyage from Thorpness, England, to Bear Island, James Bay, 13 June 1698 to 23 August 1698. [6 pages]
10. Letter by Kelsey dated Albany, 5 September 1701 [1page]
11. Memorandum describing Kelsey's service for the Hudson's Bay Company, 1683 to 1722. [4 pages]

In the commentary which follows I have tried to identify where Kelsey travelled, drawing upon the work of many persons who have grappled with this problem, to draw attention to his main observations, and to provide selected background information.

1. Journey to the Plains: The First Year, 1690

Kelsey's verse prologue provides a very quick summary of his journey from York Fort to the plains, starting in 12 June 1690. He travelled with Indians who had been to York Fort to trade. The contrast of Shield, park belt, and grasslands is clearly brought out, and a phrase such as "This wood is poplo ridges with small ponds of water" gives a good impression of undulating ground moraine on the plains. Deering's Point, named after Sir Edward Deering, Deputy Governor of the Hudson's Bay Company, is the critical hinge location in Kelsey's travels, and there has been much debate over its location. It is generally agreed that it is located beyond the Shield in the flat lower Saskatchewan River basin near The Pas, Manitoba, perhaps at a great bend in the Saskatchewan River itself, or a point on the shore of one of the numerous lakes near The Pas. It is impossible to pin Deering's Point down from Kelsey's journals, and, indeed, scholars have only brought it somewhere close to The Pas by referring to commonly used Indian routes in the region, and the more easily identifiable routes taken by Anthony Henday and Matthew Cocking when they travelled with Indians in later years.

The verse account of Kelsey's first summer of travel was written after the journey, perhaps during the first winter in the interior. It is more contemplative and reflective than his other journals. Kelsey is quite frank about his emotional state, a solitary European travelling in a strange distant land with changing numbers of Indians, searching for and meeting other Indian communities. It is natural that Kelsey would be fearful of going on a long sojourn with the Native people, isolated from his fur trade compatriots at Hudson Bay except for one exchange of messages. Helping overcome this apprehension was his genuine interest in and appreciation of Native inhabitants, and this respect remained with him throughout his career. The journey was only made possible by Kelsey becoming part of an Indian community and, as much as possible, its life during his stay in the interior. He is expressive about his annoyance and shock that the Home Indians slaughtered some of the very Plains Indians he had hoped to persuade to come to trade with the HBC. He ends this short report in verse with a description of the countryside, including the first recorded observations by a European of buffalo (bison), and the plains grizzly bear on the present-day Canadian Plains. This verse epistle is an important text of early Canadian literature.

2. Journey on the Plains: The Second Year, 1691

It is not known where Kelsey wintered in 1690-91, but from HBC records quoted in the Parliamentary Papers and from minutes in the HBC's archives it is known that in the spring of 1691 he sent a letter from the interior to Governor Geyer with Indians travelling to York Fort to trade, informing him of what he had accomplished in his first year and what he needed. At Deering's Point he received new supplies brought from York Fort by the returning Indians. It is instructive to list the things which were sent out in 1691. Kelsey had brought out a similar cargo in 1690. Some of the goods of 1691 were cached, and these are listed in the journal, but most were carried on the journey on foot through the plains, to be given as presents as appropriate:

> 1 long Eng. Gun, l short ditto l red striped blanket
> 1 present coat & cap, 2 silke sashes, 30 lb powder
> 60 lb shot, 30 lb brazile Tobacco, 50 fflintes, 12 knives
> 1 yd 3/4 broad cloath Laced, 30 Awles, 40 bells, 6 lb beads,
> 4 Hatchets, 2 Ice Chissells, 1/2 lb Vermillion, l lb red Lead,
> 1 brass Kettle wa. 6 lb l dagger, 2 pr. sissers 2 Leather
> Looking Glasses, 2 Tin Showes, 8 neck Jewells, 2 scrapers,
> 3 Ivory Combs, 4 worms, 1 pr. handcuffs 2 scaines Twine
> 4 ffire steels, 1 steele Tobacco box, 6 guilt rings,
> 2 net Lines, 1 Large powder horn & 1 moose skin
> (A.M. Johnson in Davies, 1965: 384)

In 1691 Kelsey was instructed by the governor "to search diligently for Mines, Minerals or Drugs of what Kind soever, and to bring Samples of them down with him" (Rich and Johnson, 1957: 115). It is from Deering's Point that Kelsey set out on his journey of 1691, his second penetration into the plains.

The journal of the trip into the plains in the summer of 1691 is in the form of a daily log, beginning 15 July, carefully recording the mileage covered each day, and the main events of the journey. At the start he had to catch up with the Stone (Assiniboine) Indians with whom he was to spend the summer. Having been re-supplied with goods for gifts, his objective during his summer travel was to meet other bands in the interior, particularly the Naywatame Poets, and invite and induce them to come to the Bay to trade. From 15 July to 18 July they travelled by canoe, likely on the Saskatchewan and up the Carrot River, then cached some goods to be picked up the next spring, and continued on foot. It is obviously very difficult to estimate miles travelled, especially moving with a band, but the daily progress as indicated by Kelsey ranges from six to thirty miles (9.7 to 48.3 km) when they are travelling. Kelsey's experience as a mariner may have helped him estimate distances reliably. On most days on the plains twelve to twenty-five miles (19.3 to 40.2 km) were covered, a good pace when you are travelling as a small community living off the land. We get a very good sense of the country from the items recorded in the daily journal: rivers, woods, the kinds of trees, hills, when it rains, animals, the results of hunting, a "mineral" outcrop. It is significant that a Cree place name is mentioned; naming means a land is home, and Kelsey, moving with Indian bands, was travelling in their land with them and living as they did in their home. As the community travels, it is evident how the people look after one another in obtaining and sharing food. It is apparent as well from the daily entries how important women are in carrying goods and in preparing the meat when men have killed deer or bison. We learn about shortages of food, success in killing partridges, deer, and bison, and the funeral ritual when a man dies. C.S. Houston identifies the pigeons Kelsey shot on 24 July as passenger pigeons (Houston, 1993: 27). On 12 August there is a wonderful description of park country, "Now we pitcht again & about noon ye ground begins to grow [barren] heathy & barren in fields of about half a Mile over Just as if they has been Artificially made with fine groves of Poplo growing round ym," then on 20 August they reached the grasslands, "To day we pitcht to ye outtermost Edge of ye woods this plain affords Nothing but short Round sticky grass," on 22 August he uses the term barren ground as they entered a forty-six mile (74 km) plain, "Now we pitched into the barren ground it being very dry heathy land & no water but here & there a small pond so we came to but could not see ye woods on ye other side," and on 30 August he refers to "high Champion land" in an area of poplar, birches and ponds. He probably meant "champaign land," that is, a relatively open area in generally wooded country.

Kelsey is trying to reach the Naywatame Poets, probably a Siouan-speaking tribe, an enemy of the group he is travelling with, but he repeatedly emphasizes the need to establish peaceful relations amongst the Indians of the Plains, which of course would be a great advantage to the trading enterprise of the Hudson's Bay Company. He even tries to use the bargaining lever that the governor at York Fort would refuse to trade if they do not comply, but Kelsey's arguments in the end do not carry much weight. As his group moves through the plains and woods many other Indian communities are encountered, and messages are sent as needed to neighbouring groups to arrange meetings. One has a feeling that a good network of communications exists on the plains, with messages flowing back and forth. Certainly, Kelsey's presence in the interior was widely known. He refers to an Indian who could serve as an interpreter, and Kelsey's group did succeed in reaching the Naywatame Poets and talking with their leader, but with little success in encouraging trade. In the very last entry, that of 12 September, Kelsey tells of his attempt to persuade the Naywatame Poets to travel to York Fort, and then continues directly to state that in fact they did not come to Deering's Point, "the place of resortance," the following spring, because there had been fighting and killing during the winter, and the Naywatame Poets felt they would not be safe from attack.

Kelsey's descriptions of his travels tend to be uneven because a tradition of what ought to be included in an explorer's report had not developed as yet. That emerged in the next century and a half. Nevertheless, his experience as a mariner probably led him to write his report in the form of a ship's log, describing his spatial progress day by day. The log itself would have been difficult to keep on a daily basis, because Kelsey was not a master trader in a canoe, well served by voyageurs, but travelling by himself with Indians, walking, carrying a load, and hunting, and he would have only the end of a busy, often exhausting, day to enter his observations. Kelsey, of course, had no broad areal sense of the land; that could only come later from the descriptions of Indians who knew the length and breadth of their country from their constant travels, after many traverses by explorers, and the creation of relatively permanent paper maps from such information. However, there is sufficient descriptive detail of the land in Kelsey's journal that persons who know and have studied the ground can conjecture where he travelled. In 1928 Charles Napier Bell, President of the Historical and Scientific Society of Manitoba, who in the 1870s as a young man had travelled the Carlton Trail by Red River cart and seen the plains before general agricultural settlement, proposed a route which has been broadly accepted. He also interviewed railway surveyors and government officials who knew the country first hand. Bell thought that Deering's Point was located at Cedar Lake southeast of The Pas, part of the Saskatchewan River system, and that the Indians and Kelsey travelled a short distance along the Saskatchewan and up the Carrot River, and then journeyed on foot generally southward into the Touchwood Hills area and the headwaters of the Assiniboine River (Bell, 1928). Bell's interpretation was supported by Kelsey's use of the place name, Waskashreeseebee, Cree for Red Deer River. This identifies the present river of that name which flows eastward between the Pasquia and Porcupine Hills into Red Deer Lake and on to Lake Winnipegosis. This broad region is classic morainic park-belt country and corresponds to Kelsey's description of that landscape in his entries of early August 1691, quoted above, and it is close enough to the grasslands of the plains that he could enter them and catch the quality of that distinctive landscape, described in the entries of mid- and late August 1691, also quoted above.

Many persons are intrigued by early land explorers' reports, and attempt to recapture their routes on the ground. The Rev. James W. Whillans in the 1950s tried to re-trace Kelsey's route, interviewing many old-timers who knew the land at the time of agricultural settlement (Whillans, 1955). The prairie landscape is so rich in its diversity that it seems possible to fit Kelsey's descriptions into many particular landscape niches, and this is what happened to Whillans, who time and time again imagines Kelsey striding across a particular rise or following a particular stretch of river. Whillans argues for a westward trajectory along a route south of the main Saskatchewan River, then along the South Saskatchewan, crossing it north of present Saskatoon, and ending somewhere near the Battle River. Whillans is to be commended for his research on the land, but a real problem with his interpretation is that Kelsey says nothing about crossing such a major stream as the South Saskatchewan. Charles Bell's argument that Kelsey moved southward from the Saskatchewan River toward the headwaters of the Assiniboine still appears to be soundest, and has been examined most closely on the ground by Allen Ronaghan. He has made a brilliant key interpretation of Kelsey's entry of 6 August 1691 (Ronaghan, 1984: 27-29, and Ronaghan, 1993: 90-91). Ronaghan identifies the north-south trending valley containing a small lake from which one stream flows northward and another southward, as the valley containing the headwaters of the northward-flowing Etomami River and the southward-flowing Lillian River. The well entrenched valley on the backslope of the Porcupine Hills is a glacial spillway, approximately 1 km wide, and up to 60 m deep, with an underfit stream (that is, of much smaller size than the river which first eroded the valley) meandering across the wide flat bottom. The interfleuve, described as one lake by Kelsey, consists today of two small lakes with a marsh between them. It is located near present Usherville. The Etomami flows into the Red Deer River and the Lillian into the Assiniboine. Today, a Canadian National Railway line follows the north-south valley, and Saskatchewan Highway No. 9 parallels it on the high land to the east. The valley gently grades into the plains on the south. Ronaghan suggests that on these plains Kelsey travelled as far as the Yorkton area of today, likely making some excursions into the Beaver and Touchwood Hills when he writes about the Indians catching numerous beaver in districts of woods and ponds. Ronaghan sums up his argument very effectively: "In my opinion the country south of Hudson Bay fits the Kelsey journal better than any other: a valley lying roughly north and south; rivers running both north and south from a divide; a sudden change in the appearance of the terrain; an open plain; a wooded country with many small ponds" (Ronaghan, 1993: 91).

There is no evidence of a log similar to that of 1691 for the 1690 travels. I assume Kelsey kept a log, and that it is lost. Instead what we have is the general account in verse, which covers a wide variety of topics and is a remarkably comprehensive and effective summary because it catches the highlights so effectively. What is missing in both reports is a systematic account of the two journeys, going and returning, through the Shield, except for some remarks in verse on the rivers and falls met with on the way out. Nor is there any information on where and how Kelsey spent his winters in the interior.

Sadly, Kelsey in later years apparently did not write a retrospective account of his two-year journey; if he did it has not survived.

3. Beliefs and Customs of the Plains Indians

At the conclusion of Kelsey's descriptions of his journeys in the interior there is a short account of the beliefs and customs of the interior Indians, based on his two years with them. He proceeds very systematically, plunging abruptly into a discussion of six main aspects of their customs and life, starting with the description of a feather headdress which it is believed will save a warrior from being killed in battle; going on to the rituals associated with pipes, pipe stems and smoking in preparing for war or hunting; the ritual for getting answers to questions through a medium; ceremonial singing and actions for healing sick persons; special good fortune objects carried by hunters when there are shortages of food; singing, dreaming and gods. Kelsey has comments on the role of women in the community, the different fates of men and women after death, and the ritualistic importance of allocating different pieces of meat to men and women.

Kelsey obviously asked questions, because he says that he discoursed about heaven with some Indians. He must have written this account shortly after his return to York Factory, perhaps even in the interior during his last winter there, because before his last entry he states he will discuss the Stone Indians first because he has been with them of late. He then goes on to describe rituals in their tents involving sweetgrass. This is also where he notes that though there are some differences between the Stone Indians (Assiniboine) and the Nayhaythaway (Cree) with respect to their rituals in the tents, the principles of their beliefs are the same.

In future years, published accounts of explorers' journeys in North America always contained long descriptions of the lives, customs, and beliefs of the inhabitants. Kelsey's report is the first on the life of the Natives of the western interior of Canada, and it is based on two full years living with them.

4. Journey into the Barren Grounds, 1689

This is an account of Kelsey's journey northward from Churchill along the coast of Hudson Bay, to bring the northern Indians (the Chipewyan or Dene) to trade. The journey started out by ship 17 June 1689, and likely the intention was to land at some suitable point and travel inland on foot to contact Indians in the interior who would have furs for trading. The coast was inhabited by Inuit, who also travelled inland seasonally to hunt land mammals for food and skins. Since the ice in mid-June was still so thick in Hudson Bay that the ship only got twenty leagues north of Churchill River in ten days, Kelsey proposed he be dropped on the coast where he would continue on foot. Kelsey, who was 22, was accompanied by the Indian boy who had been his companion on his walk from York Fort to Severn and back the previous winter.

Kelsey kept a careful record of the journey and its events in a daily log. They started walking 27 June. The distances covered each day ranged from five to a maximum of twenty-four miles (8 to 38.6 km), commonly between ten to eighteen miles (16.1 to 29 km). They got perhaps as far as 200 miles (322 km) north of the Churchill River, somewhere near present-day Arviat. Clearly they were beyond the tree line right from the beginning, because they did not even have enough wood to make a mosquito smudge on their second night on the land, nor any wood to contrive temporary shelters. The word barren is used, and also that aching phrase of people from forested lands, "no woods in sight." This was a new landscape, indeed, and Kelsey writes of the "coat of moss," and also of "going as if it were on a Bowling Green." The two travellers used moss to make a shelter from the rain. This is unforgiving terrain and the words rocky, hilly, and stones are constantly used. They were never far from the coast, but not right on it, where fog was encountered. Kelsey is the first European to describe the musk-ox, which he calls buffillo, and the two young men killed one. Kelsey's companion, a northern Indian [Chipewyan] was afraid of the Inuit who might be in the area. He refused to continue forward after two weeks of walking because his people would have moved too far northward to be reached. Food was no problem; on one occasion on the walk back they killed nine "deer" (caribou). After a difficult crossing of the river where they had been dropped off by the ship, they continued southward; Kelsey wrote the welcome words "To day ye woods appear in sight," and that night they were able to find adequate shelter. After one month travelling on the land they got back to the Churchill River and the ship on 28 July. This was an endurance walk, possible only for a young man in fine physical shape. To ease their loads on their return walk they left behind their trading goods, powder, shot, two ice chisels, and four hatchets, evidence of what heavy burdens they had been carrying over this hard terrain. There were dangerous crossings of rivers toward the southern end of their journey; logs were available to fashion makeshift rafts, but Kelsey still had to swim across one river because there was insufficient wood to build a raft big enough for two men. It is no surprise that this land came to be called the Barren Grounds.

During the summer of 1689 a fort was being constructed at Churchill River. After his return to the ship, Kelsey and others went by boat to fetch some things he had left behind on the coast, and while they were gone for six days this post burned down. No attempt was made to re-establish it for twenty-eight years.

5. Letter to Mr. Smith, 1694

Inserted in the journals at this point is a short letter Kelsey wrote in 1694 from York Fort to Mr. John Smith, a Hudson's Bay Company committee man in London, informing him that he has arrived safely. He states that "I shall neither do nor act on any discovery until I receive further orders from my masters in England." This experienced traveller was not asked to do any further exploring, but in his last years working for the Company, when he was governor at York Fort, he ordered exploring voyages by ship along the west coast of Hudson Bay, seeking minerals and hoping to expand trade, and led two of them himself. Apparently Mr. Smith had asked Kelsey to keep a journal, and Kelsey responds that this will be impossible because he is "likely to [be] abroad as much as at home." This simply emphasizes Kelsey's accomplishment in keeping journals on his two great earlier journeys. However, despite what he told Mr. Smith, Kelsey did manage to keep a journal at York Fort from shortly after his arrival until the French captured the fort.

6. Passage from England to the Vicinity of Cape Farewell, 1696

Kelsey made six journeys from England to Hudson Bay, and he reproduces part of the journal of his third passage out, leaving Gravesend in England on 2 June 1696, and continuing the journal until 19 July. This was the period of the English-French naval and shore conflicts in Hudson Bay. The French have taken York Fort and the English intend to take it back. Three Hudson's Bay Company ships (Kelsey was on the frigate *Hudson's Bay*) and two Royal Navy warships headed to Hudson Bay. Fish are bought from fishing boats in the North Sea; they speak to other ships and are told of French privateers; a Swedish ship informs them that Pierre LeMoyne d'Iberville has sailed with three ships; and the naval ships, sailing in what could be considered a convoy, tow some of the HBC ships as needed at various times. Every day Kelsey records sailing conditions, especially the wind (as one would expect), and reports on the sails which are used. It is very much a mariner's log. On 17 July they were fifty leagues from Cape Farewell, the southern tip of Greenland, and two days later the journal stops abruptly. The ships continued on to Hudson Bay, and from other sources we know that they arrived in August and recovered York Fort.

7. Daily Life at York Fort, 1694

The two great rivers, the Nelson and the Hayes, flow into Hudson Bay fairly close together; the peninsula separating them is about nine km across at the location of York Fort. The fort was on the north bank of the Hayes, about ten km upstream from the coast of Hudson Bay, where the river was 1.4 to two km wide. The Nelson, the much larger stream, sometimes known as the Portnelson, is six km wide roughly opposite York Fort at the later harbour of Port Nelson, and sweeps open to a width of twenty-four km at the Bay. Shoals are common in both river bottoms. On the south side of the Hayes there are a number of tributaries not far from York Fort, including Ten Shilling Creek and French Creek. Fourteens River, often referred to as "the fourteens" in Kelsey's 1696-97 York Fort journal, appears to be present-day Machichi River, flowing into Hudson Bay just east of the mouth of the Hayes, about thirteen km from York Fort. There are low islands in the Hayes River, and marshland is abundant in this whole area.

Kelsey's title for this journal of "wintering" at Hayes River is clearly incorrect. He begins the journal on 13 August 1694, a few days after his arrival at York Fort from England where he had been since September 1693, after his first term of service, and it ends abruptly less than two months later on 4 October 1694, when the fort was surrendered to the French. There are a few gaps in the journal. Kelsey was 27 years old, and had ten years experience on Hudson Bay. In the first entry we learn that the ships which brought Kelsey and the supplies and trading goods from England were departing. The usual more routine life of a post on the Bay could begin. He was sent across the Hayes River from the Fort to hunt geese for the winter food supply. He lived in a tent, and his shot and powder were replenished from the Fort by boat, by which the geese were sent back. Guns were also sent back for repair, so we infer that they were not very durable. On 14 September Kelsey returned to the Fort, and Indians out hunting brought news that two ships were seen in the Nelson River. They turned out to be French, and their commander was Iberville. On 16 September arms fire was exchanged between the French and the English, and over the next two weeks the French maneuvered their ships and landed their cannon and mortar. Occasionally the two sides fired on one another. Finally, on 3 October the French had their heavy guns ready and threatened to "reduce it [the Fort] to ashes & give us no quarter." The English governor, Thomas Walsh, surrendered the Fort the next day, with Kelsey and another man acting as his emissaries under a flag of truce. Kelsey mentions in the description of this engagement that the French have Mohawks with them. From other sources we know that after the surrender Kelsey and the Hudson's Bay Company men were the prisoners of the French for the winter, surviving as best they could in the woods under harsh conditions. Kelsey was sent as a prisoner to France during the following navigation season, and after his release was back in England by January 1696, where he rejoined the HBC and came to the Bay once more in 1696, on the voyage described in the journal before this one.

At the end of this journal there is a list of financial accounts, as in any journal of miscellany, with no seeming connection to the events above.

8. Daily Life at York Fort, 1696 to 1697

This account of wintering at York Fort from 18 September 1696 to 3 September 1697, is by far the longest of the journals. The pages recording 22 June to 1 July 1697, are torn out. The journal, as it happens, covers an interlude of one year between two French occupations. The English had just retaken York Fort from the French in August 1696, stayed one year, and then in September 1697, the French recaptured it. This was Kelsey's second experience of capitulation at York Fort.

The journal is made up of the short daily entries characteristic of all Hudson's Bay Company post journals. It may have been Kelsey's draft for the preparation of a fair official copy, with a few entries by others when Kelsey was away from the Fort. Kelsey refers to himself as "I," but when he is away the journal continues and he then is referred to as Mr. Kelsey until his return. The journal records the changing activities of the seasons; the daily recurring entries are about the weather and the food supply.

The fascination of reading this journal is in the detail describing the flow of life at an important HBC post: the ships depart for England in mid-September leaving the post isolated from Europe for a full year; the buildings and palisades are prepared for winter; there is the constant need to bring in food, be it partridges, rabbits, deer, geese, or fish; a regular trade for meat with the Indians is kept up, food is provided to Indians in need; the welcome break in routine in hunting beaver for pelts and game for food is apparent; cutting firewood, sawing planks and conveying them to the fort after spring breakup keeps the men busy; work goes on rebuilding parts of the fort after the French occupation; boats have to be refitted in spring for moving men and materials; there are the usual occasional quarrels at the post, and the inevitable deaths and burials when there is a large complement of servants; and then in spring the hectic climax of fur trading begins when tens of Indian canoes quickly arrive at York Fort after breakup, having sped down the Hayes, and the traders have to prepare the furs for the arrival of the ships and the annual shipment to England.

In the weather reports the state of the sky and the wind direction and force are invariably recorded, as befits a mariner. There are distinctive phrases such as "thick wind." Temperature is mainly ignored, even in the depth of winter, when two men are badly frozen. Some breaks in the winter cold are mentioned, for example when it is a bit milder in January and there is some melting at the end of February, or there is a hot day in July. Rain, snow, hail and frost are never overlooked. White frost is mentioned in August, but there is no hint of the existence of frozen ground. On 29 September Kelsey reports that Indian shoes were handed out to the men. These must be moccasins for winter use, an example of Europeans adopting Native ways to survive. Snowshoes are also made. The ice on the Hayes River breaks up on 16 May 1696, and this is when life changes abruptly at the Fort.

Provisions have been brought out from England, and there are references to oatmeal, pease and flour. On a few occasions Indians bring in meat in exchange for oatmeal, which illustrates the cultural exchanges at work. There is great dependence on wildlife for the basic food supply. Throughout the year partridges (grouse and ptarmigan) are shot almost every day, even in the depth of winter, and rabbits as well. Geese are first reported in late April, and then as they migrate north are shot in increasing numbers until the migration stops in mid-May. A goose tent is set up in the marsh close to the Fort, and up to 400 killed geese are accumulated at a time, all brought to the Fort. Ducks and swans are also mentioned. News is anxiously awaited in the Fort about whether deer (caribou) are passing, and there is occasional trading for deer meat. In mid-winter seventeen Indians are equipped with ten days provisions to hunt deer, and Kelsey and other HBC servants occasionally go out hunting. This particular year there is no great success. Fish are another important source of food, particularly in summer. Snow is cleared in spring from the garden, one assumes to ensure that the ground will dry more quickly, but we learn no more. Fowl, fish, and deer, the main sources of food, are what receive attention. Wolves are mentioned, and a whale shot by Kelsey, but there is no notice of polar bear or seals.

York Fort is a very active place. It had just been returned once again from the French when the journal begins, and buildings are put in repair for the winter, cracks are pointed (caulked), palisades are repaired, and then in spring there is much work in rebuilding the cook room, fixing the defence platform, rebuilding a chimney, and remounting the mortar and cannons. Wood is essential for survival; not only is York Fort made of wood, but wood is needed for heating. There is much activity over the winter at Ten Shilling Creek and another river called "the fourteens" where wood is cut for fuel and planks are sawed. Both these rivers are across the Hayes, a short distance respectively up and down that river from the Fort. The smith in the fort is kept busy repairing guns and hatchets, and making shot. After the struggle to keep warm and obtain food over winter the tempo of life changes in March. Snow is removed from platforms, the store room is cleaned, the trading room is readied for summer, and carpenters work on the boats. Once the river ice is gone, boats are in constant use to get across to the goose tents in the marshes, and to the wooding areas to raft down the planks and firewood. The river banks are slumping and stones are brought by boat to stabilize them.

There is constant trading during the year for food the Indian hunters bring in, which keeps the post lively. These are the Cree "Home Guard" Indians, but there are also a few of the Mohawks in the area who were originally associated with the French. We learn of individual Indians, including Whiskers who made himself *persona non grata* by hanging around the post with his family. The first Indians arrive by canoe to trade on 17 May, only one day after the river ice breaks up, permitting canoes to come to the fort. In May and June, fifteen to twenty canoes of Indians arrived in a single day to trade, stay one day or a little longer and leave. There are up to fifty canoes at the Fort at one time. The arrivals fall off in mid-June, but a few canoes still come in early July. Different Indian groups who have arrived are mentioned, including the Stone (Assiniboine), Upland, and plain Indians, the latter arriving only in July. The plantation is the flat area along the river bank extending toward the fort where Indians camp for a few days when at the fort to trade. Then they head back upstream to their home territories. For the Englishmen it is true that life is hard on the Bay, but as one reads one cannot help thinking of the Indian canoes arriving at York Fort after an exceedingly long and arduous journey. Each canoe has travelled, perhaps fifteen to twenty days across the Shield with much portaging. The Europeans are relatively passive collectors of furs at the Bay.

But Kelsey is anything but passive. Not only had he made his great journeys in earlier years, but even here at York Fort he is out and about. In winter he is deer hunting north of the Nelson River from 23 February to 30 March, and in spring at the goose tents from 13 to 17 May. This is apart from many one-day or overnight excursions, and a trip by shallop from 15 to 22 July along the coast between York Fort and the mouth of the Severn to retrieve a beached boat reported by Indians.

Three days after Christmas, in the entry for 28 December 1696, Kelsey writes a sentence in Cree which he annotates in English, "A pleasant fancy of old time which made me write in an unknown tongue because counsel is best kept in one single Breast," meaning that it was for his eyes alone. In "Henry Kelsey's Christmas

Message," David Pentland, with the aid of Cree associates whom he gratefully acknowledges, has translated this as "Everyone is drunk because of the celebrations. I'd like to fetch a woman [or my woman]. I always have trouble [?] sleeping. If only I could see her, I'd be able to sleep, even if I got into trouble the same night" (Pentland, 1991: 128). Pentland discusses the custom of celebrating Christmas at fur trade posts with alcohol. He also considers the likelihood that Kelsey had earlier taken an Indian wife, and this is thought to be plausible, though she was apparently no longer with him in 1696.

In the summer of 1697 the conflict on Hudson Bay between the English and the French resumed; a fleet of three English ships, including one warship, and a French fleet of four warships under Iberville headed for Hudson Bay and York Fort. In a naval battle in the shallow estuary of the Nelson River Iberville in his own ship, the *Pelican* defeated the English fleet, even though his other three ships were not on hand. After the victory the *Pelican* was lost in a storm in shoal water, but the crew was saved, and using his other ships and crew Iberville landed his force and cannon on the shore of the Hayes River. This is the point at which Kelsey's journal takes up the account of the fight in the last days of August. On this occasion there was a battle at the Fort. There was skirmishing and firing of mortar and cannon, with the bombs and balls going both ways, and at least one HBC servant was killed. Kelsey reports that there were 900 French. In the end, after an exchange of messages on surrender terms, Kelsey and two others carried Governor Henry Baley's letter of surrender to Iberville, and once more he and many others were shipped off to France, apparently in the same navigation season (1697), so that this time he did not winter as a prisoner on the Bay. From France he was allowed to return to England, once more to rejoin the service of the HBC. It must have been frustrating to have worked all year refurbishing the Fort after the previous French occupation, do one season's trading, and then have everything fall into the hands of the French once more. But that was the ongoing story of the duel between the French and the English here on the waters and shore of Hudson Bay until the Treaty of Utrecht (1713) finally put an end to these maneuvers and the English gained undisputed possession of the lands on the Bay, including York Fort.

Kelsey's feelings are well expressed by his concluding words: "this being ye end of a Tedious winter & tragical Journal by me Henry Kelsey."

9. Passage from England to James Bay, 1698

Two Hudson's Bay Company ships, the *Deering* and the *Perry*, left Thorpness on the east coast of England just north of Ipswich on 13 June 1698, for Hudson Bay. Kelsey was in the *Deering*, once more travelling to Hudson Bay after having been captured by the French. In the North Sea they traded for fish with the doggers (fishing boats) on the fishing banks. Kelsey's log is much more detailed on latitude and longitude, bearings, distance travelled each day, and even the depth of water in Hudson Bay, than his log on the 1696 voyage. By 20 June they had reached "Dunkins head," probably Duncansby Head on the northeast coast of Scotland, and then there is a gap in the log from 21 June to 9 August as they cross the Atlantic Ocean and pass through Hudson Strait.

The log begins again on August 10 at "cape diggs," either the cape in northwestern Québec which marks the entrance to Hudson Bay, or the cape at the eastern end of the Digges Islands, also in that area a short distance off shore, known today as Cape Digges. There were still ice floes in the Bay. As they navigated through broken ledges of ice they saw a polar bear on the ice on 10 August, not far from "cape diggs," and on 17 August they saw a seal on the ice. From 17 to 21 August they had to sail carefully amongst the ice floes. Kelsey used Bear Island in James Bay for an orientation point as recorded in his log, and the journal ends 23 August while they are still aboard ship heading southward to Albany on James Bay. Since the French held York Fort, known by them as Fort Bourbon, from 1697 to 1714, the Hudson's Bay Company's sole posts during those years were on James Bay, with the operations centred at Albany Fort, and it is on James Bay that Kelsey worked for the Company during that period.

10. Letter Dated Albany Fort, 5 September 1701

This letter is written to Kelsey's superiors in England. At this time Kelsey was master of the ship *Knight*, responsible for expanding the fur trade at the bottom of James Bay in the face of rival French traders from the south, and he was also the chief trader at Eastmain. He explains how he was delayed in getting to Eastmain, thereby missing the Indians who came to trade there, because his ship was ice-shoved on a high bank at Bayley's Island during spring breakup of the lower Albany River. "Slude river" is present-day Riviére Eastmain. As well as summarizing his activities, Kelsey asks for a raise of £10 for doing work two men did previously.

11. Kelsey's Summary of His Activities for the Hudson's Bay Company 1684 to 1722

This is a chronological listing, with descriptive comments, of Kelsey's career with the Hudson's Bay Company, from the time he was first employed by the Company in 1684 (in error he writes 1683) to the time of his retirement in 1722. It was a long career. Some entries are very brief, but others are full and throw light on his responsibilities and accomplishments. We learn of his efforts while he was in charge of Eastmain on the east side of James Bay to develop the trade in that area. There is considerable descriptive detail of his actions as an experienced mariner in rescuing the cargo of a HBC ship grounded at Albany in 1711. Then in 1719 when he was governor of all the posts on Hudson Bay he describes how he sailed north along the west coast of the Bay to inspect the "Eskimoe" country, at which time he exchanged two young slaves (Indian captives) for two young Eskimoes (Inuit) to acquire interpreters and learn more about the country. Later that year he almost lost his life when a HBC ship foundered in shoal water near York Fort and he supervises the transfer of the cargo to shore. In 1720 he ordered a ship to explore northward and bring the two Inuit back to their people, and we learn that the two Indians they had been exchanged for were dead. This ship reported on the area on the northwest coast of Hudson Bay where James Knight's two ships, sailing from England, had been searching for the North-West Passage. Knight's hope was that the Passage would lead them to the elusive gold mine thought to lie somewhere in the northern Barren Grounds, but the ships were not seen. Knight's ships, which we now know were moored at Marble Island where the expedition was wintering, were both crushed in the ice, marooning the crews, and all died on the island, most likely of scurvy and by starvation. In 1721 Kelsey sailed for the Eskimoe country along the west coast of Hudson Bay searching for copper. Strong winds prevented him from reaching Marble Island where Knight's ships were lost, although they saw objects from the vessels, presumably among the Inuit they encountered. Later in 1721 Kelsey tells of helping navigate a HBC ship safely into Hayes River in dangerous circumstances. Apparently a vicious storm broke out in the shoal waters of the estuary after he had gone aboard the ship, and the Captain of the vessel then deliberately set it adrift in order that Kelsey would have the authority by maritime convention to take over as master and bring the ship to safety. The impression one is left with is that navigation was extremely hazardous for sailing vessels in Hudson Bay. In Kelsey's later years with the Company overcoming maritime misadventures must have been highlights of his life on the Bay. The memorandum ends abruptly in 1722, the year he retired and left Hudson Bay for good.

Kelsey's retrospective of his life is very laconic about his early exploits, the very achievements for which he is renowned today. The later sections describing voyaging along the coast take on the length and detail of reports to his superiors.

BIBLIOGRAPHY

Bell, C.N. 1928. "The Journal of Henry Kelsey (1691-92)." *Transactions* (New Series), No. 4. The Historical and Scientific Society of Manitoba, Winnipeg.

Davies, K.G., ed. 1965. *Letters from Hudson Bay 1703-40.* Vol. 25. The Hudson's Bay Record Society, London.

——. 1969. "Kelsey, Henry." In *Dictionary of Canadian Biography. Vol. 2, 1701-1740,* 307-15. University of Toronto Press, Toronto.

Dempsey, James. 1993. "Effects on Aboriginal Cultures Due to Contact with Henry Kelsey." In Epp, *Three Hundred Prairie Years,* 131-35.

Doughty, A.G. and C. Martin, eds. 1929. *The Kelsey Papers.* King's Printer, Ottawa.

Epp, Henry, ed. 1993a. *Three Hundred Prairie Years: Henry Kelsey's "Inland Country of Good Report."* Canadian Plains Research Center, Regina.

——. 1993b. "The Life: Animals and their Importance to Humans." In Epp, *Three Hundred Prairie Years,* 35-37.

Gibson, Terrance H. 1993. "Whom Kelsey Met: Lifestyles and Technology of the Late-Seventeenth-Century Cree." In Epp, *Three Hundred Prairie Years,* 95-112.

Glover, Richard, ed. 1962. *David Thompson's Narrative.* Vol. 40. The Champlain Society, Toronto.

Great Britain. 1749. *Papers Presented to the Committee Appointed to Inquire into the State and Conditions of the Countries Adjoining to Hudson's Bay, and of the Trade Carried on There.* Parliament, House of Commons, London.

Houston, C.S. 1993. "The Life: Bird Observations." In Epp, *Three Hundred Prairie Years,* 27-34.

Johnson, Alice A. M. 1960. "Henry Kelsey." In Davies, *Letters from Hudson Bay,* 376-94.

Kenney, James F. 1929. "The Career of Henry Kelsey." In *Transactions of the Royal Society of Canada.* 3rd Series, 23(2), 37-71.

Morton, Arthur S. 1939. *A History of the Canadian West to 1870-71.* Thomas Nelson and Sons Ltd, London.

Payne, Michael. 1989. *The Most Respectable Place in the Territory: Everyday Life in Hudson's Bay Company Service York Factory, 1788 to 1870.* (Studies in Archaeology Architecture and History.) Canadian Parks Service, Environment Canada, Ottawa.

Pentland, David H. 1991. "Henry Kelsey's Christmas Message 1696." In H.C. Wolfart, ed.,

Linguistic Studies Presented to John L. Finlay, 127-38. Memoir 8. Algonquian and Iroquoian Linguistics, Winnipeg.

Rich, E.E. 1958. *The History of the Hudson's Bay Company 1670-1870. Vol. 1: 1670-1763.* The Hudson's Bay Record Society, London.

Rich, E.E. and A.M. Johnson, eds. 1957. *Hudson's Bay Company Copy Booke of Letters Commissions Instructions Outward, 1688-1696.* Vol. 20. The Hudson's Bay Record Society, London.

Robson, Joseph. 1752. *An Account of Six Years Residence in Hudson's Bay, from 1733 to 1736 and 1744 to 1747.* J. Payne and J. Bouquet, London.

Ronaghan, Allen. 1984. "Kelsey's Journal of 1691 Reconsidered." *Saskatchewan History* 37, no. 1: 25-31.

——. 1993. "Reconstructing Kelsey's Travels." In Epp, *Three Hundred Prairie Years*, 89-94.

Ruggles, Richard. 1991. *A Country so Interesting: The Hudson's Bay Company and Two Centuries of Mapping 1670-1870.* McGill-Queen's University Press, Montreal/Kingston.

Russell, Dale R. 1993. "The Puzzle of Henry Kelsey and His Journey to the West." In Epp, *Three Hundred Prairie Years*, 74-88.

Thistle, Paul C. 1993. "Dependence and Control: Indian-European Trade Relations in the Post-Kelsey Era." In Epp, *Three Hundred Prairie Years*, 124-30.

Tyrrell, J. B. 1931. *Documents Relating to the Early History of Hudson Bay.* Vol. 18. The Champlain Society, Toronto.

Warkentin, Germaine. 1991. " 'The Boy Henry Kelsey': Generic Disjunction in Henry Kelsey's Verse Journal." In I.S. MacLaren and C. Potvin, eds., *Literary Genres/Genres littéraires*, 99-114. Research Institute for Comparative Literature, Edmonton.

Whillans, James W. 1955. *First in the West: The Story of Henry Kelsey, Discoverer of Canadian Prairies.* Applied Arts Products, Edmonton.

Wolfart, H. Christoph and David Pentland. 1979. "The 'Bowery' Dictionary and Henry Kelsey." In William Cowan, ed., *Papers of the Tenth Algonquian Conference*, 37-42. Carlton University, Ottawa.

INTRODUCTION TO THE 1929 EDITION

Arthur G. Doughty and Chester Martin

(a) The Kelsey Papers

In the year 1926 certain documents were presented to the Public Record Office of Northern Ireland by Major A.F. Dobbs, of Castle Dobbs, Carrickfergus. These had been collected by Arthur Dobbs, author and statesman, who in addition to displaying varied interests, and no small influence, in colonial affairs during the eighteenth century — he was Governor of North Carolina from 1754 until his death in 1765 — distinguished himself as a critic of the administration of the Hudson's Bay Company.

In the Dobbs Collection were found *The Kelsey Papers*, now classified in the Public Record Office of Northern Ireland, Belfast, as D.O.D. No. 162, and here published jointly by the Public Record Office of Northern Ireland and the Public Archives of Canada. These papers — journals, letters and memoranda — are, it seems probable, in the handwriting of Henry Kelsey himself. A comparison with his signature attached to certain letters in Hudson's Bay House is, however, inconclusive. The text here used was transcribed from the original under the supervision of Dr. James F. Kenney of the Public Archives of Canada. Dr. Kenney has also seen the present volume through the press.

The Kelsey Papers are in one volume of 128 pages, in a coarse paper cover, probably the original binding. At the top of the first page, in the same handwriting as what follows, is the title "Henry Kelsey his Book being ye Gift of James Hubbud in the year of our Lord 1693." In that year Kelsey was in England — he had returned from Hudson Bay in 1692. Who James Hubbud was we do not know.[1] It seems probable that Kelsey's words record merely a gift of a blank copy-book from a friend. It is obvious that the majority of the texts which follow are transcripts, and the probable inference is that they were copied by Kelsey for his own private use, the originals going into the files of the Hudson's Bay Company. The first document in point of time is the Churchill *Journal* of 1689, but the rhymed introduction to that of 1691 has first place in the manuscript volume.

How *The Kelsey Papers* came into the possession of Arthur Dobbs is not now known, and it would be rash, perhaps, to conjecture. The last entry in them is of date 1722, and Dobbs's controversy with the Hudson's Bay Company began only after Kelsey's death. Internal evidence in Dobbs's own writings is fragmentary and almost altogether negative. In Dobbs's book of 1744 — *An Account of the Countries adjoining to Hudson's Bay* — there is no reference to Kelsey. It seems safe to say that he knew nothing of his papers at that time. By 1749, on the other hand, Dobbs had not only heard of Kelsey but was prepared to impugn the whole account of him which the Company had prepared for the Parliamentary Committee of that date. In the *Dobbs Collection* is a manuscript *Commentary on the Case of the Hudson's Bay Company as presented to the Committee of 1749.* This is in the handwriting of Arthur Dobbs himself, and it is followed so closely by Robson in his *Account of Six Years*

Residence in Hudson's-Bay, 1752, Appendix I, that a common origin seems self-evident. It is possible that Dobbs's *Commentary* is a paraphrase of Robson, made at some period between 1752, when Robson's book was published, and 1754, when Dobbs left for North Carolina. Internal evidence, on the other hand, indicates the reverse, for the Robson *Appendix* shows the marks of careful literary craftsmanship. Both agree, however, upon the story that appeared in print for the first time in Robson and formed the foundation, as we shall see, of a Kelsey tradition which has survived in one form or another for nearly 200 years. Impugning the Company's claim to have sent Kelsey to the prairies upon a journey of discovery, Dobbs charged that "Geyer [the Governor at York Fort] did not send him up, but that upon some Boyish misbehaviour he had been severely corrected by the Governrs. orders and being very great [*sic*] and Intimate with the Indians he took an opportunity of running away with them; so that Geyer finding the Company desirous of sending up upon Discoveries made Merit of his going up and said he sent him up." This story Robson claims to have heard during his stay of six years on Hudson Bay — a tradition which we must presently examine. It will be conceded that this story could scarcely have survived an honest examination of *The Kelsey Papers.* So too with other details of the *Commentary* which Dobbs must have added in good faith. He charges that Geyer "did not comply with their former Instructions" of 1688 to send Kelsey to the Churchill — "which was not Done [he adds] and no reason assigned for that neglect." *The Kelsey Papers* prove not only that the instructions were complied with but that the Churchill journey was made, and recorded in minute detail, by Kelsey himself. The meagre conclusion may perhaps be allowed that *The Kelsey Papers* came into Dobbs's possession only when his bitterest attacks upon the Company were being abandoned. Did they contribute in any degree to that result?

(b) The Kelsey Tradition

The true story of Henry Kelsey supplants a myth which has been in historical currency for nearly two hundred years — a curious instance of cumulative prejudice and inaccuracy.

Since Robson's *Account of Six Years Residence in Hudson's-Bay*[2] the claim of the Hudson's Bay Company that Kelsey was sent by them "to travel and to penetrate into the Country," and that he "chearfully undertook the Journey," has been met with incredulity. The tradition arose that Kelsey was "but a boy" who had run away from the harsh discipline of Governor Geyer at York Fort at the mouth of the Nelson; and that the Company "made a merit of Kelsey's going up" by fabricating the garbled pages of his *Journal* in order to conceal their failure to explore the vast regions claimed by their Charter. "From many circumstances mentioned in this journal," wrote Robson, "I no more believe that it is Kelsey's than it is mine."[3] This story has since been embellished with much ingenuity, both in fiction and in sober history. *The Kelsey Papers* now supply not only the truth about the journeys of 1690-2 but an outline, at times in great detail, of Kelsey's activities from the time he entered the service of the Company in 1684 to the year 1722, four years after he became Governor of York Fort.

The name of Henry Kelsey[4] appears for the first time in print in the *Report* of the British Parliamentary Committee (April 24, 1749) "Appointed to enquire into the State and Condition of the Countries adjoining to Hudson's Bay."[5] This enquiry was the outcome of one of the most determined attacks ever made upon the Hudson's Bay Company as to the validity of their Charter. After fourteen years of agitation, the voyage of the *Dobbs-Galley* and the *California* had been, in 1746-7, undertaken by public subscription for the discovery of the North-West Passage. In this project Arthur Dobbs, in whose library at Castle Dobbs, Carrickfergus, were found *The Kelsey Papers*, was undoubtedly the moving spirit; and his own book, *An Account of the Countries adjoining to Hudson's Bay*, published in 1744, sufficiently illustrates his motives. Another shareholder was Henry Ellis, afterwards Governor of Georgia, friend of William Knox the confidant of Grenville and Lord North, and for a time Governor of Nova Scotia (1761-3) after the death of Lawrence. Ellis's account in *A Voyage to Hudson's-Bay*,[6] published in 1748, and two volumes published by William Drage, "Clerk of the California" in 1749,[7] attest the public interest as well as the less disinterested motives of Dobbs and his associates in the contest against the Company. In 1748 a petition found its way to the law officers of the Crown, and to a Parliamentary Committee. The burden of the petition was for "the like Privileges and Royalties as were granted to the said Company"; and the main charge was that "they have not discovered, nor sufficiently attempted to discover, the Northwest Passage into the *South Seas*."[8] It was in rebuttal of this charge that the Company submitted what purported to be "A JOURNAL of a Voyage and Journey undertaken by *Henry Kellsey*, to discover, and endeavour to bring to a Commerce, the *Naywatamee Poets*, 1691."[9]

The *Journal* was accompanied by circumstantial evidence. Preceding it in the *Report* (Appendix No. XXVII) are excerpts from letters between the Company and various Governors on the Bay from May 9, 1676, to June 4, 1719.[10] As early as 1683 Governor Sargeant was instructed to "choose out from amongst our Servants such as are best qualified with Strength of Body and the Country Language, to travel and to penetrate into the Country." "For their Encouragement, we shall plentifully reward them." Nothing, however, could induce them to stir from the Bay. Sargeant reported in 1685 that neither the four men specifically chosen "nor any of your Servants will travel up the Country." Finally in June, 1688, the Company directed Governor Geyer to send "the Boy *Henry Kelsey* ... to *Churchill* River with *Thomas Savage*, because we are informed he is a very active Lad, delighting much in Indians Company, being never better pleased than when he is travelling amongst them." How did this "very active Lad" first attract the notice of the Company? Who was "Thomas Savage"? Was Kelsey sent to the Churchill? How did he come to undertake the journey to the prairies in search of the "Naywatamee Poets"? The answers to these questions, as we shall see, are to be found for the first time in *The Kelsey Papers*.

But there were several features of the *Journal* which invited suspicion, and the fact that the enemies of the Company were allowed to exploit these with impunity was taken in itself as *prima facie* evidence. The title of the *Journal* appears in triplicate and the text in duplicate in the *Report* of 1749. The first title in the *List of the Appendix* (p. 236) and in the text (Number XXVII, p. 273) was evidently intended to cover all the evidence submitted by the Company with regard to Kelsey. It reads: "A JOURNAL of *Henry Kellsey* in the Years 1691, and 1692, sent by the *Hudson's Bay* Company to make Discoveries, and increase their Trade Inland from the Bay." Number XXVIII is "A JOURNAL of a Voyage and Journey undertaken by *Henry Kellsey*, to discover, and endeavour to bring to a Commerce, the *Naywatamee Poets*, 1691." It is dated "July the 5th." Under the same number in the Appendix is a "Duplicate" dated "July 15th, 1692" — obviously the same journal with trifling variations in both title and text. The first closes with the words, "Sir, I remain, Your most Obedient, and Faithful Servant, Henry Kellsey"; the second, "I rest, Honourable Masters, Your most Obedient, and Faithful Servant, At Command, Henry Kellsey." Assuming that the Company and not the printer was responsible for these irregularities, Robson ingeniously implied an attempt to pass off the record as "two journals; one in 1691 in compliance with the governor, and the other in 1692 in obedience to the Company."[11]

It is noteworthy that neither Arthur Dobbs, among whose papers at Carrickfergus *The Kelsey Papers* were found, nor Ellis and Drage, so far as we know, ever impugned the Kelsey *Journal* in print, though Dobbs in his *Commentary* (already noted) is as sceptical as Robson himself with regard to its authenticity. It is noteworthy, too, that Dobbs had no comment whatever to make on Kelsey before the Parliamentary Committee (p. 228). In 1752, however, Joseph Robson — also a witness in 1749 — in his *Account of Six Years Residence in Hudson's-Bay*, attacked not only the authenticity of the Kelsey *Journal* but the *bona-fides* of the Company's correspondence. Robson was a stone-mason — he built much of Fort Prince of Wales at Churchill — who wrote under the title of "Late Surveyor and Supervisor of the Buildings to the Hudson's-bay Company." How Umfreville, who wrote in 1790, could refer to him as "a candid, true, and impartial writer"[12] it is hard to understand. Both, however, had quarrelled with the Company. In truth, Robson's rancour against the "sea officers principles" in vogue at Hudson Bay is self-evident in his own scathing narrative, and he himself suggests that the Company induced him to go to the Bay the second time (1744-7) "to keep me from Mr. Dobbs."[13]

The account which Robson professed to have received from "the servants in the Bay" was as follows:

> *"Henry Kelsey, a little boy, used to take great delight in the Company of the natives, and in learning their language, for which, and some unlucky tricks that boys of spirit are always guilty of, the governor would often correct him with great severity. He resented this deeply; and when he was advanced a little in years and strength, he took an opportunity of going off with some distant Indians, to whom he had endeared himself by a long acquaintance and many little offices of kindness.*
>
> "A YEAR *or two after, the governor received by an Indian a piece of birch-rind folded up, and written upon with charcoal. This was a letter from Kelsey; in which he intreated the governor to pardon him for running away, and to suffer him to return with favour and encouragement. Accordingly he came down with a party of Indians, dressed after their manner, and attended by a wife, who wanted to follow him into the factory. The governor opposed this; but upon Kelsey's telling him in English, that he would not go in himself if his wife was not suffered to go in, he knew him, and let them both enter. Many circumstances of his travels were related: that the Indians once left him asleep; and while he slept, his gun was burnt by the fire's spreading in the moss, which he afterwards stocked again with his knife: that he and an Indian were one day surprised by two grizzled bears, having but just time to take shelter, the Indian in a tree, and Kelsey among some high willows; the bears making directly to the tree, Kelsey fired and killed one of them; the other, observing from whence the fire came, ran towards the place; but not finding his prey, returned to the tree, which he had just reached when he dropped by Kelsey's second fire. This action obtained him the name of Miss-top-ashish, or Little Giant.*
>
> "WHEN *Kelsey was afterwards made governor of Yorkfort, I was told that he wrote a vocabulary of the Indian language, and that the Company had ordered it to be suppressed."*[14]

Robson's criticism of the correspondence in the *Report* of 1749, and of the

Journal itself, it will be unnecessary to examine here.[15] "Sufficient to discredit the whole," he concluded, was Kelsey's claim to have followed a party of Indians over the prairies several days behind them: "computing, I suppose, the number of men, the weight of their bodies, the size of their feet, and the angle of each step."[16] It is but fair to add that many of the embellishments of the Kelsey myth have been added since the pages of Robson were written in 1752. Such is the havoc wrought by prejudice when unhampered by the discipline of historical evidence.

(c) Kelsey's Own Story

The Kelsey Papers supply for the first time a fairly comprehensive outline of Kelsey's activities from 1683 to 1722. Why they close in 1722 we shall, perhaps, be able to conjecture.

The eleven journals, letters, memoranda, etc., in the series cover a wide range of interest. They explain the Company's choice of Kelsey as early as 1688 for the task of inland discovery. It has been assumed that the Churchill project of that date was never undertaken. Kelsey's own journal of 1689 now supplies in detail the story of that ill-fated enterprise. The journal of 1691, too, is found here unabridged, with a rhymed introduction by Kelsey himself — perhaps the most valuable pages of the entire series, since they fix approximately the location of Deering's Point, whence the journeys of 1690 to 1691 began, and prove beyond reasonable doubt that Robson's story, impugning alike the good faith of the Company and the achievements of Kelsey himself, was a groundless fabrication. With the location of Deering's Point, the range of Kelsey's memorable travels — the preliminary journey of 1690 and the more ambitious project of 1691 — is brought within the bounds of reasonable conjecture. The five closely packed pages of Kelsey's *Acco^t. of those Indians belief and Superstitions,* is the first outline, if we are not mistaken, of the life and customs of the plain Indians.[17] Beyond a doubt Kelsey was the first white man to reach the Canadian prairies and to see the plain Indians hunt the buffalo.

The *Journal* of 1694 with the surrender of York Fort "to Mr. Diberveall" on October 4, and that of 1696-7 with the second surrender to Iberville on September 3, 1697, are of great historical interest. For sixteen years after the Treaty of Ryswick in that year the hold of the Company upon the Bay came almost to an end. For Kelsey himself the autobiographical notes at the close of *The Kelsey Papers* — *"Memorandum of my abode in Hudsons bay from 1683 to 1722"* — will explain many tantalizing problems raised by the vagaries of the Kelsey tradition, leaving others, however, still unsolved among the mysteries of those eventful years.

Why the *Memorandum* closes at August 16, 1722, it is possible, perhaps, to conjecture. Despite the prevalent tradition to the contrary, the decade following the Treaty of Utrecht, which re-established the Company's hold upon the Bay, were years of great activity. In 1719 Captain Knight with the *Albany* and the *Discovery* had sailed away to the northward, never to return. Nearly fifty years later a whaling-ship found the wreck upon the bleak rocks of Marble Island. For months, the Esquimaux said, the survivors, crazed with hunger and solitude, fought for their lives against the wolves and the cold, scanning the horizon in vain, day after day, for a sail.[18] On June 1, 1720, the Company had written to Kelsey, then Governor at York Fort, "to send us Copies of all those Journals that have been kept by yourself and others, and what Discoveries have been made in the Voyages to the Northward."[19] At the same time Kelsey was submitting to the Company his own "Design of Wintering to the Northward." The following year, as he notes in his *Journal*, he had "Intentions of going farther to ye Noward to look for ye place where ye albany sloop was lost we seeing things belonging to those vessels." The Company, however, countermanded Kelsey's design of "Wintering farther Northward [than Churchill], to the Hazard of your Life, and those with you," but they despatched the *Whalebone Sloop* to be "sent upon Discovery next Year [1722], as soon as the Season of the Year will permit," and to return by "the Beginning of September."[20] Kelsey's last memorandum is dated August 16, 1722, when the "*Whalebone* came in here from Churchill." It seems reasonable to suppose that the last date in *The Kelsey Papers* is related in some way to Kelsey's final project of northern discovery in 1722 and to the Company's request for "Copies of all those Journals that have been kept by yourself." Was the "Duplicate" *Journal* published in the *Report* of 1749 taken from these "Copies" of 1722?

But the problems at this point begin to multiply. The *Journal* of 1691 in *The Kelsey Papers*, with its rhymed introduction for the voyage of 1690, is from "Henry Kelsey his Book being ye gift of James Hubbud in the year of our Lord 1693." At this time Kelsey himself was in England.[21] How did *The Kelsey Papers*, here published, find their way into the possession of Arthur Dobbs? What happened to Kelsey after 1722? He must have been well over 50 years of age at that time, but gallant old Knight was over 70 when he undertook the ill-starred expedition which ended at Marble Island. Much, as we shall see, is to be found in the papers of Hudson's Bay House to supplement the meagre knowledge of Kelsey's movements after 1720. He was recalled in 1722, under certain charges that were never, it seems, pressed against him. He applied for another command in 1724 but the ship he applied for was not that year sent to the Bay. In 1730 Mrs. Kelsey was a widow applying for pension. These details and many others are to be gleaned from the *Minute Books* and *Letter Books* of the Hudson's Bay Company. Under this category they will be noted presently in greater detail. But the whole story of Kelsey's closing years will perhaps be known only when the treasures of Hudson's Bay House can be systematically classified, and carefully searched for this purpose.

The chief revelations in *The Kelsey Papers* must be sought in detail in the papers themselves. A very brief summary must suffice here by way of introduction. Curiously enough the earliest detail fixed by Kelsey is found to be an error. "In 83," he writes, "I went out in ye ship lucy Jno. Outlaw commandr." We are indebted to Mr. Leveson-Gower of Hudson's Bay House for evidence that the *Lucy* came to Hudson's Bay only in 1684. How Kelsey attracted the notice of the Company is stated as follows: "In 88[22] after 3 indians being employ'd for great rewards to carry letters from hays river to new severn they return'd w^th^out performing ye business altho paid then was I sent wth an indian boy & in a month return'd wth answers." It was "ye same Indian boy" under the name of "Thomas Savage" who accompanied Kelsey on the ill-fated Churchill expedition of 1689, for on June 2, 1688, the Company had directed that "the Boy *Henry Kelsey* be sent to *Churchill* River with *Thomas Savage*, because we are informed he is a very active Lad, delighting much in Indians Company, being never better pleased than when he is travelling amongst them."

The Churchill *Journal* is a grim story of hardship and failure. Striking inland "about 20 Leagues from Churchill River," (June 27) Kelsey and his lone companion marched over barren lands with "abundance of Musketers" and with "no shelter but ye heavens for a Cannope." On July 9 he "spyed two Buffilo" (musk-oxen) with horns that "Joyn together upon their forehead & so come down ye side of their head & turn up till ye tips be Even with ye Buts their Hair is near a foot long." Thus Kelsey, it would seem, is the first white man to see the musk-ox. After 128 miles he found a decided "backwardness" in "Thomas Savage," who "told me," adds Kelsey, "I was a fool & yt he would go no further for I was not sensable of ye dangers." Returning to Churchill they found that the house then being built for the trade "was Reduced to ashes and yt most of ye things were Burnt." At York Fort, concludes Kelsey, "I went to ye Govern^{r}. taking ye Indian Boy wth me & acquainted him how I had been serv'd by him ye Governors reply was yt I had my labour for my travell since yt ye Governr. Never did Require any further acco^{t}. of me."

The next year, however, (1690) Governor Geyer had a harder task for Kelsey. "This Summer," he wrote, "I sent up *Henry Kelsey* (who chearfully undertook the Journey) up into the Country of the *Assinae Poets*, with the Captain of that Nation, to call, encourage, and invite, the remoter Indians to a Trade with us." In 1691 came "a Letter from *Henry Kelsey*, the young Man I sent up last Year with the *Assinae Poets*." The Governor had sent Kelsey "a Supply of those Things he wrote for," and had ordered him "to return the next Year, with as many Indians as he can." In September, 1692, Geyer wrote that Kelsey had come down "with a good Fleet of Indians." This is the record in the *Report* of 1749, and it is now corroborated in great detail by *The Kelsey Papers*.

"Ye Compy.", writes Kelsey, "employed 2 french men viz, Gooseberry [Groseilliers?] & Grammair ... to go amongst ye Natives to draw ym to a trade but they did not go 200 miles from ye factory upon wch. I was sent away wt ye stone Indians in whose Country I remained 2 years."[23] In the rhymed introduction to the *Journal* of 1691, Kelsey is still more explicit:

"In sixteen hundred & ninety'th year
I set forth as plainly may appear...
And for my masters interest I did soon
Sett from ye house [York Fort] ye twealth of June
Then up ye River I with heavy heart
Did take my way & from all English part
To live amongst ye Natives of this place
If god permits me for one two years space
The Inland Country of Good report hath been
By Indians but by English yet not seen...
Gott on ye borders of ye stone Indian Country
I took possession on ye tenth Instant July
And for my masters I speaking for ym all
This neck of land I deerings point did call
Distance from hence by Judgement at ye lest
From ye house six hundred miles southwest
Through Rivers wch run strong with falls
thirty three Carriages five lakes in all."

By September he had passed through wood of "small nutts wth little cherryes very good ... till you leave ye woods behind:"

"And then you have beast of severall kind
The one is a black a Buffillo great
Another is an outgrown Bear wch. is good meat...
He is mans food & he makes food of man...

This plain affords nothing but Beast & grass
And over it in three days time we past...
It being about forty sixe miles wide...
At deerings point after the frost
I set up their a Certain Cross
In token of my being there
Cut out on it ye date of year
And Likewise for to veryfie the same
added to it my master sir Edward deerings name."

The second journey from Deering's Point (1691-2) is traced in detail in Kelsey's own *Journal*. After paddling for three days and a half from July 15 — 71 miles, the last day up a "Stream Running very strong" — Kelsey and his party left the river and followed "ye Stone Indians wch were gone ten days before." During a journey of 55 days, over more than 500 miles of swale and prairie, Kelsey describes how the Indians killed "great Store of Buffillo"; how the "Naywattamee poets," having killed three of the Nayhathaways, had "fled so far, that ... I should not see them"; how he met the Stone Indians from the south on August 25, so "in number we were 80 Tents"; how Kelsey at a feast on September 3 gave the Governor's message that he would not "trade with ym if they did not cease from warring"; how messengers came at last from the "Naywatame poets"; how he made peace between them and the Stone Indians, and finally on September 12, after presents and an elaborate powwow, got a promise from the Naywatamee chief to come to the Bay. The variations between the printed *Journals* of the Report of 1749 and the unabridged *Journal* of the Kelsey Papers are by no means slight, but there are no discrepancies that are not easily explained. Thus is Governor Geyer at last vindicated.

In the autumn of 1692 Kelsey returned to England. In 1694 he came back to Hudson Bay but "was taken by ye french and brought home." The story in detail appears in Kelsey's letter of August 8, 1694, and in his *Journal* from August 13 to October 4.[24] Iberville with two French ships arrived on September 14, landing 30 or 40 men, with "mortar pieces" and "Boom shels"; on October 3 came an ultimatum under a flag of truce, that they were "ready to Cannonade and Boombard ye fort & if we would not surrender it they would reduce it to ashes & give us no quarter." Next day the Governor decided to surrender, and with "14 more of us was ordered to go up to Mr. Diberveall." Again Kelsey went to the Bay in 1696 for "ye retaking ye fort again"; but "Mr. Diberville ... wth. 3 Saile" was not to be caught. Next year came the famous actions between the *Pelican* and the *Hampshire, Hudson's Bay* and *Deering*. A second time Iberville landed with mortar and bomb. Three times his demands were "denyed"; but in the end, "finding such great force as nine hundred men and ye ill tidings of our own ships," the garrison "marcht out ... & ye french took possession of ye fort this being ye end of a Tedious winter & tragical Journal by me Henry Kelsey."

A third time Kelsey returned to the Bay in 1698. In 1701 he is "master of ye ship and factory" at East Main; in 1703 he is in England again; in 1706 he comes out as "mate of ye perry frigte" — his taste for seamanship now dominant in his journals — and trader again to East Main. He is back in England in 1712; returns to the Bay when the French claims are forever set at rest in the Treaty of Utrecht; and in 1718, at last, becomes Governor of his old post at York Fort. He is busy with his projects for discovery and "Wintering to the Northward" when the curtain falls upon his adventurous career in *The Kelsey Papers* in 1722. The rest of his life must be pieced together from other sources. There seems to be no record of his return to the Bay after his recall in 1722, and it seems safe to say that his bones rest in English soil.

Much that we should like to know about Kelsey is as elusive as the mist which he once described at York Fort. The precocious courage of "the Boy *Henry Kelsey*" is never belied during the forty years, nearly, of his recorded life. In his Churchill journey "Thomas Savage" called him a fool because he was "not sensable of ye dangers"; and when they had to build a raft, to cross the river for their return, "it would not Carry us & the goods," adds Kelsey, "so put ye Boy & things on it & swim'd over it my self being very cold." In his great venture of 1690 he "was resolved this same Country for to see"; though he added with the truthfulness of real courage, that he had "often been oppresst":

"Because I was alone & no friend could find
And once yt in my travels I was left behind
Which struck fear & terror into me."

Robson himself, as we have seen, passes on the tradition that he once killed two grizzly bears on this journey to the prairies, and that the Indians admiringly called him "Miss-top-ashish, or Little Giant" — almost the only note we have of his stature or personal appearance. When the *Whalebone* and *Prosperous* "rid a very hard storm" in 1721, the captain "would have me taken charge of his vessel," and "thank god," adds Kelsey modestly, "we gott both very well in." It was Kelsey who salvaged the *Perry's* cargo and the "Seafords pinnace." His stout preparations during the "tedious winter" of 1696-7 — the "palisadoes," the "brasspieces," the "big morter," and the "flankers" — were in keeping with his bearing with "Mr. Dibberveal" as he closed his "tragical Journal" in the following September.

There is more of discretion than of humour in *The Kelsey Papers;* and that, perhaps, is to be expected. On the last day of the old year, 1696, he writes half a dozen lines of Indian dialect[25] in his *Journal* — as a "pleasant fancy of old time ... because counsel is kept best in one single Breast. Vale." To keep the Stone Indians from the warpath, he notes, "all my arguments prevailed nothing ... so I seeing it in vain held my peace." He has his jest, too, at the medicine-men who know what "ye firmament of heaven is made of," since they "have been there and seen it." Even the interminable monotony of "patridges," and "wooding" at "the Fourteens," and "goose tents" in the marshes, and "telling Beaver into ye warehouse" at York Fort, is not altogether unrelieved by the fortunes of "Whiskers" and his indigent progeny.

(d) Kelsey and the Company

The material relating to Henry Kelsey is so meagre that even the most commonplace fragments may be worthy of record. The details in the *Minute Books* and *Letter Books* of the Hudson's Bay Company, and in the *Journals* of the posts on Hudson Bay, are frequently prosaic — records of salary paid or agreed upon, appointments made, results commended or criticized. But many have an interest little anticipated when these formal entries were made, while some of them are fairly charged with history. It may be advisable to collect a few of these items here in chronological order for purposes of record.

Henry Kelsey entered the service of the Hudson's Bay Company as an apprentice on April 14, 1684. He was at this date, it would seem, 14 years of age. In that case the year of his birth was the year of the Hudson's Bay Charter. His first engagement was for a period of four years, at the end of which he was to receive the sum of £8.0.0 "and two shutes of apparell."[26]

On May 2, 1684, there is an entry in the *Minute Book:* "Paid to John Butlaw for disbursements for Henry Kesley as one of the Compa. apprentices £5.12.0."

Four years later, on June 2, 1688, the instructions, afterwards quoted in the *Report* of 1749, were issued to Governor Geyer: "That the Boy Henry Kelsey bee Sent to Churchill River with Thomas Savage because Wee are Informed hee is a very active Lad Delighting much in Indians Compa. being never better pleased then when he is Travelling amongst them."[27] Nothing further is noted of the Churchill journey, but when Geyer reported (September 8, 1690) "This summer I sent up Henry Kelsey (who chearfully undertook the Journey) up into the Country of the ASSINAEPOETS with the Captain of this Nation," the Company replied (May 21, 1691) that they were "glad you prevailed with Henry Kelsey to undertake a Journey with the Indians to those Remote parts hopeing the Encouragemt. you have given him in yt advance of his Sallery will Instigate other young men in the factory to follow his Example."[28] This "advance of his Sallery" must refer to the new engagement at the end of Kelsey's four years of apprenticeship, in 1688, for the journey to the prairies in 1690-2 was to be rewarded by Governor Geyer at his discretion. "We are glad," the Company wrote on June 17, 1693, "that Henery Kelsey is safe returned and brought a good fleet of Indians downe with him and hope he has effected yt wch he was sent about in Keeping the Indians from warring one with another, that they may have the more time to look after theire trade... As for the Service Henery Kelsey has done us in traveling up into the Countery you being imediate Judges of his demerits we leave it to your discretion to gratifie him for the same."[29]

On April 25, 1694, Kelsey, who was then, as we have seen, in England, was engaged by the Company at a salary of £30 per annum. On May 30, 1694, there is a letter from the Company to Captain Knight: "Wee have delivered to Kelsey one gun made by Capt. Silke 4 foote long which he is to use in ye voyage and is to deliver into the ffactory at his arrivall."[30] In 1698 Kelsey was re-engaged for a period of three years at a salary of £25 (£5 less than his previous salary) "But upon Gouvr. Knights recommendation of his Fidelity and diligance in all respects," adds the Company, "to have £5 per annum more advanced to him."[31] It is fair to add that this was just after the disastrous Treaty of Ryswick when retrenchment was the order of the day. Kelsey's share in the recapture of York Fort in 1696, futile though it proved to be, was acknowledged by the Hudson's Bay Committee "on Board the Dering ffrigtt. at the Nore" on May 31, 1697. "We thanke God," they wrote, "for the success you had last yeare in Retakeing Yorke ffort."[32]

During the lean years between the Treaties of Ryswick and Utrecht, 1697-1713, Kelsey's name appears frequently in the records of the Company. On June 23, 1702, the committee acknowledged Kelsey's "Letter of 5 Sept. last and are well Satisfied with Gouvr. ffullertines makeing you Master of the Knight and Sending you to the East Maine."[33] Three years later the *Minute Book* (November 28, 1705) contains the entry that "Mr. Henry Kelsey was now Entertained in ye Compies. Service Upon the following Agreemt. Vix [*sic*] to goe with ye Compies. shipp next

Expedition for Hudsons Bay as Cheife Trader in the Country and to have ye Sallary of Deputy Gouvr. Vix [*sic*] £100 p Ann from his Arivall in ye Country and if Mr. Bishop should be Dead, Then to Succeed Him as Deputy Gouvr. but if Liveing then Mr Kelsey to be Cheife Trader at Albany Fort."[34] By a Minute of the Committee, duly signed by the Governor and Deputy Governor, Kelsey was made "Comdr. of ye Knight ffrigte as likewise cheife Factor at ye East Maine."[35]

In the year 1707 there are various references to Henry Kelsey in the *Journals* of Anthony Beale of Albany Fort; and a payment of £5 was made on May 14, 1707, to Henry Kelsey's wife.[36] The *Knight*, on which Kelsey sailed in 1707, failed to reach East Maine "By Reason of Sundry accidents falling out," but the Company "Were glad to hear of your Safe arriveall there and also Recd. your Journall in your outward bound Voyage which wee approve well off."[37] In the year 1709 there is a payment "to Mrs Eliz Kelsey, wife of Henry Kelsey" of £28.8.2, and in 1710 another of £30.[38]

A letter from the Governor in Committee on May 29, 1710, is of more than passing interest. Kelsey was advised to act solely under the direction of the Governor at Hudson Bay: "without his Consent you are not to act anything upon your owne head and must observe to allow him to have the casting voice ... You doe well to Educate the men in Literature but especially in the Language that in time wee may send them to travell If wee see it Convenient... As for discoveries of mines etc it is noe time to thinke upon them now In times of Peace Something may be done... We have sent you your dixonary Printed that you may the better Instruct the young Ladds with you, in ye Indian Language."[39] Is Kelsey's proposal "to Educate the men in Literature" the first note of a long tradition of good books at the Hudson's Bay posts? And is Kelsey's "dixonary Printed" the first indigenous literary product of Rupert's Land? This is evidently the "vocabulary of the Indian language" to which Robson characteristically refers in his *Account of Six Years Residence in Hudson's-Bay*: "When Kelsey was afterwards made governor of York-fort, I was told that he wrote a vocabulary of the Indian language, and that the Company had ordered it to be suppressed."[40]

In 1711 there are casual references to Kelsey in Anthony Beale's *Factory Journal* at Albany Fort, and on August 1, 1712, the entry that "Capt Ward and Henry Kelsey sail on Board Knight bound for England."[41]

With the Treaty of Utrecht, 1713, the fortunes of the Company were at last restored. Two entries of this period are of great interest. For May 20, 1713, the Company's *Minute Book* contains the following record:

> *"Mr. Henry Kelsey now gave in his Proposals to serve the Company as Deputy Governour at Port Nelson, under Capt. James Knight (viz): To be Deputy Govr. under Capt: James Knight at £100 pr Ann, & when he returns for England, or in Case of his Death, (which God forbid) I hope to succeed him.*
>
> *"I hope the Company will consider & allow me something for my being left Governour by Mr Fullertine, and if my health should not permit me to stay, then I may have the Liberty to Return by the first oppertunity, otherwise to give one Years Notice before I come Home, & the Company to allow me the Benefit of one Servant with me...*
>
> *"Which proposals of Mr. Henry Kelsey were likewise agreed to by the Committee & his Wages to Commence from his Arrival at Port Nelson."*

The other item appears in the *Minute Book* for August 14, 1713. It proves, contrary to the Canadian contentions during the next century, that the rights of the Company were not held by the Crown to have lapsed (for all but Albany Fort and East Main) by virtue of the disastrous Treaty of Ryswick,[42] but that possession was taken by the Crown in 1713, "for Us and In Our Name ... for the use and benefitt of the Govr. & Compy of adventurers of England tradeing into Hudsons Bay & their Successors":

> *"Two Commissions from Her Majesty (viz) one to Captain James Knight to be Governour, & Mr. Hen. Kelsey to be D. Governour in Hudsons Bay ... which is to be sent by ye Compies Shipp all which were now Locked up in ye Iron Chest."*
>
> *"Anne, by the Grace of God Queen of Great Britain france & Ireland Defender of the Faith &c. To our Trusty and Well Beloved Captain James Knight and Henry Kelsey Esq Greeting... To take possession for Us and In Our Name of the said Bay and Streights, Lands Seas, Sea Coasts, Rivers, Places, Fortresses and other Buildings ... for the use and benefitt of the Govr. & Compy of adventurers of England tradeing into Hudsons Bay & their Successors."*[43]

Kelsey was kept waiting in England for some time and it was not until May, 1714, that he received his Commission. For this and "the Former Services of Mr. Henry Kelsey," the Committee, "for his Encouragement Doe Agree to give him a gratuity of £75 besides the £25 Lent him by the Compa in all £100."[44] On May 28, 1714, the Secretary is instructed to have the agreement "Engraved on Stampt Paper in order to be Signed" by the Committee.[45]

In the York Fort *Journal* (7. A. 3, 1714) is a copy of Governor Knight's letter describing how he and Kelsey took possession of Fort Nelson in the summer of 1714: "Found the Fort in a most miserable condition — all Rotten and ready to Fall... One of the Indians came wn I hoisted ye Union fflag he told me he did not love to see yt he loved to See the White one So there is many of The Indians has Great Friendship for the french here."

Certain charges were made against Kelsey at this time. They were either made by Captain Knight or were transmitted to the Company by him. The letter containing the charges is not in the records, but it would appear from a letter from Kelsey to Staunton that thefts by the Indians formed the basis of the charges. On June 14, 1719, the Company wrote a private letter to Kelsey as follows:

> *"Wee Cannot but Acquaint you what Accusations have been Laid Before us Concerning yr Conduct which wee hope you will Clear Your Self of and that you may be the better able to do it have Inclos'd Sent you a Copy thereof, that You may Know Both your Accusers, and what is charg'd against You to which we desire your Answer to Every Particur being very Unwilling to think that a Person wee had so Good an Opinion of as yourself should forfeit their Estimates who are Your Loving Friends..."*[46]

Though the "Accusations" against Kelsey must have been forwarded to London not later than 1718, he remained at Hudson Bay for four years during which he was Governor at York Fort and first in command of all the posts on the Bay. For the present, at least, the nature of the charges can only be surmised. In the York Fort *Factory Journal* (15. A. 3) for February 1, 1719, is the copy of a letter from Kelsey to Staunton, then at Churchill, referring to Captain Knight's voyage of discovery that was to end in disaster at Marble Island. "Be sure you follow ye Compies Order in that affair," writes Kelsey, "for I am very sure they have done me all the prejudice lies in their Power by fals asspersions concerning ye Indians and had it not bin for ym it would been very hard wth us this winter for they have killed near 100 Deer ...

in one Paragraph of my accusations you are brought in as a Wittness by Capt Knight about you telling him of seeing the Indians in Capt Baylies time carry several Bundles out of the Trading Roome in the Night but I looke on this and the rest as the efects of their Mallice to turn me out of my Employ for no other reason then their being afraid of being out done but be it as it will it shall not lessen my endeavours nor I hope yours of doing what wee can to promote their Trade and Intrest during our Servitude in this Countrey."

A year later Kelsey wrote to Staunton: "I doe asure you that I am noways offended wth you about what I writ concerning Cap Knight but you may believe it is a great Dolor to be represented so Odiously to Our Masters and tuched in ye most Sensable part yt is a mans reputation wch is more Valuable yn Life itselfe for wch reason it ought to be very Cautiously Handled And if it please God I live to see ym shall Endeavour to make ym prove their Asertions."[47]

During this entire period Kelsey's dominant interest in the cause of "discovery to ye Norward" is to be traced in many ways. A short voyage in the summer of 1719 had promising results. "I saw many Esquemoes," wrote Kelsey, "and gott some whalebone Oyle and Some Sea Horse teeth and changed two of ye Compies Slaves[48] for two of those Countrey Ladds and they are very agreeable and learn English apace by wch I hope to know wt ye Countrey will afford."[49] Next year (June 1, 1720) the Company wrote to Kelsey as follows:

> *"Wee also Order you to send us Coppies of all those Journals that have been Kept by yourself & others, & what discoveries have been made in yr voyages to ye Northward, also what Numbers of People & what sort you have met wth, & what Quantity of Whales have been seen ... likewise from whence ye flood Comes, & from what point of ye Compass, & how Much ye Tides have flow'd up and downe."*[50]

This was followed by more stringent instructions in the following year. On May 26, 1721, the Governor and Committee wrote, evidently with some concern, of Kelsey's "designe of Wintering to the Northward." "Wee desier," they added, "to know whether you meane at Churchill River, for wee cannot Aprove of your Wintering further Northward to the Hazard of yr Life and those with you wee Aprehending if you goe anytime in June you may make as much discovery both of whales & other Comodites as if you Wintered to ye Northward & Returned by the Latter End of August And hope you may give us better Incouragement as to discovering A Trade Either be getting of Copper or any other Vallueable Comodity then wey have hitherto met with."[51]

When Kelsey was finally summoned home in 1722, therefore, it is hard to say whether the old charges about the Indians or the growing expenses from these years of fruitless "discovery to ye Norward" were uppermost in the minds of the Committee. Their letter to Kelsey (May 24, 1722) was as follows:

> *"Capt Kelsey, you having now been 8 years in our Service, 4 of which you were Dept Govr and 4 years Governor, at York Fort, Wee think it Convenient to Call you home & accordingly Expect you by ye Return of ye Mary Friggt Capt Jas Belcher Commandg. having appointed Mr Thos Maclish in your Stead, to whom you are to deliver possession of our Fort & Country, as soon as he shall arrive on Shoar, & Wee have order'd Mr Maclish, to Show you all possible Respect, untill ye Departure of our Ship for England."*[52]

From an entry in the *Minute Book* (October 31, 1722) it is clear that Kelsey was "Welcomed by the Committee on his return home." The old charges against him were never revived, or, if revived, were never proved. In the *Minute Book* of the following year (January 23, 1723) appears the following entry:

> *"This Comitte Takeing into Consideration the Skins Caught & Brought Home by Capt. Henry Kelsey & which were sold at the Comps Sale did Resolve to allow him the full Produce of his sd Skins amo to £22.13.2 The sd Capt Kelsey haveing served The Compa in Hudsons Bay as Govr & Deputy Govr for Eight Yeares Sucessively Last past which sum yr Secr is ordered to pay him."*

In the following year, 1724, Kelsey himself appears for the last time. On January 29, 1724, the *Minute Book* records that "The Severall Petitions of Capt. Henry Kelsey & Capt Geo Keneday were deld in Desireing to be Comanders of ye Comps Shipp Hannah in ye Rome of Capt. Gaston Decd The Secr is ordered to Lay them by, the Comitte Intending to appoint A day to Consider of that Matter." On February 12, 1724, the Committee "resolved not to send the Hannah to Hudsons Bay this year."

It remains to record two brief entries which tell their own poignant story. Under date of January 28, 1730, appears the following note in the *Minute Book:*

> *"Eliz Kelsey Widow of Capt Heny Kelsey late Governor for the Compa at York Fort in Hudsons Bay having Petitioned the Committe to Allow her something towards puting out her son apprentice; The Comittee takeing into consideration the former Service of her Husband the said Heny: Kelsey Ordered that the Secr do pay her ten Guineas as a Gratuity from the Compa for that purpose, £10.10.0."*

And finally, on February 20, 1734, ten years after Kelsey had applied for the command of the *Hannah*, his name appears for the last time, it would seem, in the records of the company: "Eliz. Kelsey Widow of Heny Kelsey formerly Govr for the Compa at York Fort in H. Bay haveing petitiond the Committee to give her Something to buy her son John Kelsey Cloths She being wholly incapable to do it herself this Committee considering the former Service of his Father the sd Heny Kelsey Ordered the sum of £6.6.0 to be laid out for cloths for him & that ye Secr see the same laid out."[53]

Kelsey's death must have taken place between February, 1724, and January, 1730. The fact that his widow was constrained to ask of the Company "Something to buy her son John Kelsey Cloths She being wholly incapable to do it herself" is an apt commentary upon the vicissitudes of adventure and discovery in the fur trade.

(e) Kelsey's Route in 1691

The most interesting problem, perhaps, in *the Kelsey Papers* must be left, in the last resort, to the topographer with intimate first-hand knowledge of the northland. What was Kelsey's route in the journeys of 1690-1? How far south and west did he travel in his quest for the "Naywatamee Poets"? And, finally, where was Deering's Point,

> *"Distance from hence by Judgement at ye lest*
> *From ye house six hundred miles southwest*
> *Through Rivers wch run strong with falls*
> *thirty three Carriages five lakes in all?"*

Kelsey left York Fort on "ye twealth of June," 1690, and "took possession on ye tenth Instant July" of Deering's Point "on ye borders of ye stone Indian Country." Already, he notes, "the ground begins for to be dry with wood Poplo and birch with ash thats very good." Farther on there are "small nutts wth little cherryes ... till you leave ye woods behind," and find the "Buffillo great." A year later in the same region he notes "great store of Beast," where the Indians made "a great feast telling yt they were very glad yt I was returned according to my promise."[54]

The *Journal* of this second voyage over the prairie (1691), unhampered by metre or rhyme, is more explicit. Kelsey's purpose, however, was not primarily to chart the country but to bring the Indians "to a Commerce" at the Bay. The interminable pages of nautical observations in the *Journals* of 1698 prove alike Kelsey's seamanship and his skill with compass and chart; but in 1691 he is still a very "young Man." Three years before he had been "the boy *Henry Kelsey.*" The absence of topographical detail, therefore, is easily understood. He had set forth for his "masters interest" —

> *"for to understand*
> *The natives language & to see their land."*

It is necessary, therefore, at the outset to stress three facts all of which are of prime importance in interpreting the evidence of Kelsey's *Journal* of 1691. *(a)* He left York Fort on June 12, 1690, and reached Deering's Point on July 10. For this, the first voyage of a white man by the waterways from the Bay to the Saskatchewan, Kelsey kept no journal, and the only record is the meagre rhymed introduction for the *Journal* of the following year. *(b)* After his arrival at Deerings' Point in July, 1690, he followed the Indians to the plains for the winter and returned to Deering's Point in July of 1691, to meet the Indians returning from the Bay. For this, too, the first journey of a white man upon the Canadian prairies, Kelsey kept no journal, and the only record is the same rhymed introduction, together with a few fragments of internal evidence from the *Journal* of July 15- September 12, 1691. Thus the Indians on the plains, he notes on July 30, 1691, were "glad yt I was returned according to my promise." His first reference to the buffalo, too, for 1691 is the casual note (August 19) of "ye Indians having seen great store of Buffillo But kill'd none." He was evidently familiar with the buffalo from his previous visit, and his description of both the grizzly bear and the buffalo on the following day (August 20) has all the casualness of previous knowledge. These details are almost the only evidence we have to confirm the rhymed introduction and Governor Geyer's correspondence, that a white man had found his way to the Canadian prairies in 1690. *(c)* In the third place, the *Journal* of 1691, here published in full for the first time, is after all but the third stage of Kelsey's memorable expedition to the prairies. Returning to Deering's Point in the summer of 1691, he had "Receivd those things in full wch ye Governour sent me," no doubt by the Indians returning from their annual journey to York Fort; and it was in order to follow these "Stone Indians wch were gone ten days" before him up the Saskatchewan that he began the journey with which his *Journal* opens — "taketh my depart from Deering's Point" on July 15, 1691.

Without forecasting at this juncture the location of Deering's Point, the subsequent journey may briefly be outlined from Kelsey's narrative in order to supply the necessary context. The third day after leaving Deering's Point, they decided (writes Kelsey) to "lay up our Cannoes" upon a "small arm of ye River" — a "Stream Running very strong" — and to "set forward into the woods." They travelled six days — nearly a hundred miles — before they had "very good going." That evening they overtook the Stone Indians — seven tents — who had left

Deering's Point ten days before them. Three weeks from Deering's Point came messengers from "some stone Indians ... to ye Southward of us." His rendezvous two days later is "at a place called Waskashreeseebee," a shallow stream "not a hundred yards over" which "breants [branches?] away much to ye Southward & runneth through great part of the Cuntry & is fed by a lake wch feedeth another River wch runneth down to ye Southward of us... Now ye water wch runneth down this River is of a Blood red Colour by ye description of those Indians wch hath seen it." For 25 miles they took their "Course along the Riverside it Running or lying up between ye South South west but unnavigable for either boat or Cannoe." In several places Kelsey "Saw slate mines along the side of this River." Here it was that the Indians, for the first time, "kill'd great store of Beast," leaving "the women to fetch home ye meat & Dress it ye Indians Likewise feasting & making of feasts all ye day." Seven weeks after leaving Deering's Point, the Stone and "Nayhaythaway" Indians came in touch with their enemies who "knew not ye use of Cannoes." The final powwow with the "Nawatamee" chief took place two weeks after crossing a great plain of 46 miles. In all Kelsey had travelled from Deering's Point for 59 days — an estimated distance of 585 miles. Passing the winter, no doubt, with the Stone Indians, Kelsey, for the third time, "was at Deerings point in the spring," whence, as we have seen, he went "down with a good Fleet of Indians," to York Fort, and returned to England with the Hudson's Bay ships in the autumn.

It is clear that the vital factor for the geographer must be the location of Deering's Point. With the appearance of traders — French, and, after 1763, British — from Canada, the whole routine of the Hudson's Bay fur trade is revolutionized, and the historical data of that time with regard to Indian routes to the Bay would be of little value here. Fortunately, however, there is earlier evidence which is not only very nearly contemporary with Kelsey, but fairly conclusive, it would seem, with regard to the Indian routes to the Bay.

Deering's Point is called by Kelsey "ye place of resortance when they are coming down to trade." Arthur Dobbs is at pains to quote from La Potherie,[55] and from the account of Jérémie who was stationed at Ste. Theresa (York Fort) during the French occupation after the Treaty of Ryswick in 1697, being Governor there in 1713 when it was given up again to the British after the Treaty of Utrecht.[56] According to La Potherie, "these Nations, who come from a great Distance, assemble in *May* at a great Lake, sometimes 12 or 1500 together, to begin their Voyage ... in which Time they make their Canoes, which are of Birch Bark... There comes down generally to Port *Nelson* 1000 Men, some Women, and about 600 Canoes." The Nelson (Bourbon), he adds, "takes its Source from a great Lake called Michinipi."[57] According to Jérémie, the Nelson "by which the Natives come down to trade" is of "so great Extent, that it passes thro' many great Lakes," the greatest of which "they call *Michinipi,* or the *Great Water,* because in Effect it is the greatest and the deepest Lake, being 600 Leagues in Circumference... About this Lake ... are great Numbers of Indians, who call themselves Assinibouels."[58] Again, the great lake from which the "River Bourbon" (Nelson) flows is "called, the *Junction of the two Seas,* because the Land almost meets in the middle of the Lake. The East Side of this Lake is a Country full of thick Forests, in which are great Numbers of Beaver and Elks. Here begins the Country of the *Christinaux*... The West Side is full of fine Meadows, filled with wild Oxen; the Assinibouels live here."

It is reasonable to suppose that the "Michinipi" of both La Potherie and

Jérémie is Lake Winnipeg, and that during the period of French occupation, less than ten years after Kelsey had gone inland from York Fort with the Stone Indians, they were following regularly the Nelson route (either down the Nelson to its mouth or across from Split Lake to Fox River and the Hayes) gathering each year in May at some "great Lake" for the purpose of making their canoes. Here, adds Jérémie, "Joy, Pleasure, and good Cheer reigns."

This account is curiously confirmed in great detail by the next available evidence after Kelsey's day — the story of Joseph La France, a French Indian who travelled in 1739-42 from the Great Lakes to Lake Winnipeg and Hudson Bay. Dobbs claims to have taken down La France's account "Word for Word"[59]; and beyond a doubt his description of Rainy Lake, Lake of the Woods, the Winnipeg River, and "the great *Ouinipique* Lake," is a marvel of accuracy for such a time. "Upon the West Side of Lake Ouinipique," said La France, "are the Nation of the *Assinibouels* of the Meadows." After a winter of land travel, "in which Time he passed Northwards near 100 Leagues," he found himself (March, 1742) at Lake Cariboux which descends through marshes into Lake Pachegoia,[60] which is "the Lake where all the *Indians* assemble in the latter End of *March* every Year, to cut the Birch Trees and make their Canoes of the Bark ... in order to pass down the River to *York* Fort on *Nelson* River with their Furs; it is divided[61] so as to make almost two Lakes; the West Side by which he pass'd was about 100 Leagues in Circuit; the other Side or Eastern Lake was much larger, as the *Indians* informed him. The River *De vieux Hommes* runs from the West for about 200 Leagues, and falls into this Lake ... it has a strong Current, and is always muddy... They were three Weeks in passing along the West Side of the Lake before they came to the Place it is discharged by the River *Savanne* or *Epinette*... The River was small where it came out of the Lake, for about six Leagues, it spreading through several little Passages through the Marshes, but farther down, when collected together, formed a large River." "The Banks were low, until they got to the great Fork, where the River is divided by a Rock, upon which a convenient Fort might be built, which might be cut off by bringing the Water around it." From "the Great Fork" La France descended by "the East Branch ... it being the shortest Passage; at the same time another Fleet of 100 Canoes went down the Western Branch." In this at least it is easy to recognize the Nelson and Hayes River routes to York Factory.[62]

Such are a few of the historical details which the topographer must now reconcile in tracing the overland journeys of Henry Kelsey.[63]

NOTES

1. There was an Isaac Hubbud in the service of the Company in Hudson Bay in 1689. See p. 31 *infra.*
2. Joseph Robson, London, 1752.
3. *Id.*, p. 73.
4. Journals, letters, etc., in *The Kelsey Papers* are uniformly signed "Kelsey." The *Journal* in the *Report* of 1749 is attributed to "Henry Kellsey," the spelling retained by Burpee in *The Search for the Western Sea*, pp. 96-113; the letters — no fewer than eight on pp. 254, 274-5 of the *Report* — uniformly use the form "Kelsey," and the same spelling is found in Kelsey's own letters in Hudson's Bay House.
5. *Reports from Committees of the House of Commons*, vol. II (1803), p. 213-286.
6. Ellis sailed with the expedition "in quality of *Agent* for the *Committee.*" *Voyage*, p. 104.
7. *An Account of a Voyage for the Discovery of a North-West Passage*, 2 Vols., Lond., 1748.
8. *Report*, 1749, p. 285.
9. *Id.*, p. 276. "Poets" seems to have been a suffix attached to the names of several Indian tribes as these were written by the English in Hudson Bay. Kelsey speaks of the "Naywatame Poets" and the "Mountain Poets," and in the records of the Company are found also the designations "Assinae

Poets" and "Kanebickapoets." *Cf.* Gideon D. Scull, *Voyages of Peter Esprit Radisson* (Boston: The Prince Society, 1885) p. 345.
10. *Id.*, pp. 273-6.
11. Robson, *op. cit.*, Appendix, p. 23.
12. *The Present State of Hudson's Bay*, Edward Umfreville, London, 1790, p. 4.
13. *Op. cit.*, p. 18.
14. *Id.*, p. 72.
15. "I no more believe that it is Kelsey's, than it is mine." *Id.*, pp. 72-4, and Appendix, pp. 14-25.
16. "I would not undertake to follow any track but a beaten one." *Id.*, p. 74.
17. "Having been amongst ye Stone Indians of late."
18. Samuel Hearne, *Journey from Prince of Wales Fort in Hudson's Bay to the Northern Ocean, 1769-1772*, London, 1795.
19. *Report*, 1749, p. 254.
20. *Ibid.*
21. See below, p. 112
22. Is this another error for "87"? The Company's letter about "the Boy Henry Kelsey" and "Thomas Savage" is dated, June 2, 1688 (*Report*, p. 274). It could scarcely have been written from London the same year as Kelsey's journal to New Severn.
23. *Memorandum*, 1690, See below, p. 111. By "Gooseberry" and "Grammair" are designated Jean Baptiste, son of Médard Chouart des Groseilliers, and Elie Grimard, whose names, in various and curious spellings, are found several times in the *Minutes* of the Hudson's Bay Company. On March 13, 1685, they and two other Frenchmen were "entertained in the Company's service" for four years, Chouart at £100 per annum, Grimard at a salary rising from £30 to £45 per annum.
24. See below, pp. 33, 39-45.
25. Cree, or some related dialect, but the transliteration is so uncertain that translation cannot be attempted.
26. H.B.C. *Minute Book*, April 14, 1684. Hudson's Bay House.
27. H.B.C. *Letter Book* 602, p. 5. Hudson's Bay House.
28. *Id.*, p. 43.
29. *Id.*, p. 68.
30. *Id.*, p. 103.
31. *Minute Book*, May 25, 1698.
32. *Letter Book* 603, p. 59.
33. "Wee hope and doe Expect you will be Industrious and faithfull in Dischargeing the Trust Reposed in you." *Id.*, p. 105.
34. *Minute Book*, 227.
35. *Id.*, 228, March 19, 1706.
36. *Albany Fort*, No. 2. A. 3, 1706-1707; *Minute Book*, 1707.
37. *Letter Book*, May 26, 1708.
38. *Minute Book*, March 25, 1709, and May 17, 1710.
39. *Letter Book* 603, p. 199.
40. P. 72.
41. Anthony Beale, *Factory Journal*, 3.A.3, 1711; 4.A.3, 1712.
42. See the evidence of Chief Justice Draper before the Select Committee on the Hudson's Bay Company, 1857, *Report*, p. 210.
43. The Commission is dated July 21, 1713.
44. *Minute Book*, May 4, 1714.
45. Kelsey's Commission as Deputy Governor at York Fort is in *Letter Book* 603, p. 250.
46. *Letter Book* 604, p. 59.
47. York Fort *Journal*, 15. A. 3, April 12, 1720.
48. "Two Slave Boys," in the York Fort *Council Book*, 15. A. 3, June 10. 1719.
49. York Fort *Council Book*, 15. A. 3., Kelsey to Maclish, Jan. 18, 1720.
50. *Letter Book* 604.
51. *Ibid.*
52. *Ibid.*
53. *Minute Book*. In an *Apprentice Book*, Inland I, Vol. 12, p. 171, Public Record Office, appears the following: [1731] June ye 16th [No.] 11 [Masters Names Place of Abode Trade] Thos: Fanner of

Selbourn Southton Cordwainer [Apps. Names & Fathers & Abode] Will: Son of Eliz: Kelsey [Date of Inst.] 1 May [Memoriall of Articles & Indrs:] (Common Indenture & Count. pt.) Do. [Term of years] 8 ys fr date 7.-.-. -. 3.6.

54. *Journal,* July 30.
55. *Histoire de l'Amérique Septentrionale,* Paris, 1722, 4 Vols.
56. Bernard, *Recueil de Voiages au Nord,* Amsterdam, 1724.
57. Dobbs, *op. cit.*, pp. 25, 23.
58. *Id.*, p. 20.
59. *Report,* 1749, p. 228.
60. Moose Lake, north of the Saskatchewan, and Cedar Lake?
61. It would seem that Dobbs, in taking down La France's narrative, has confused Lake Pachegoia (Cedar Lake?) with Lake Winnipeg, the west side of which from the mouth of the Saskatchewan (La France's "River *De vieux Hommes"?)* to the outlet of the Lake by the Nelson River is here so clearly described by La France.
62. Dobbs *op. cit.*, pp. 29-45. La France's narrative is reprinted in *Report, 1749,* pp. 243-8.
63. Since this was written, the above Introduction was presented in part (sections *(b), (c),* and *(e)*), together with an outline of this edition of *The Kelsey Papers,* at the opening annual meeting of the Manitoba Historical Society on February 14, 1928. Since that time Dr. C.N. Bell has prepared a paper, dealing chiefly with Kelsey's route in 1690-2, for the joint meeting of the Canadian Historical Association and the Manitoba Historical Society on May 24, 1928. This paper has since been published under the title *The Journal of Henry Kelsey, 1691-1692,* (Dawson Richardson Publications, Limited, Winnipeg) with valuable maps from Dr. Bell's own collection.

Dr. Bell's chief conclusions are *(a)* that the "Lake Cariboux" and "Lake Pachegoia" of La France are Moose Lake and Cedar Lake respectively (p. 12); *(b)* that Deering's Point must therefore be on Cedar Lake (p. 14); *(c)* that Kelsey paddled from Deering's Point up the Saskatchewan to the mouth of the Carrot River, and up the Carrot River for 28 miles before striking inland on July 18, 1691 (p. 21); *(d)* that the "Waskashreeseebee" (almost the only name mentioned by Kelsey) reached on August 1 was the Red Deer River of eastern Saskatchewan and western Manitoba, flowing into Lake Winnipegosis (p. 31); and *(e)* that Kelsey's route between Deering's Point and York Fort was by way of Moose Lake (the route of Hendry in 1754 and of Cocking in 1772) instead of the Saskatchewan to Lake Winnipeg and the Nelson as indicated so clearly from the narrative of La France.

With regard to the last, it seems remarkable that there should be no mention of the Moose Lake route for 64 years after Kelsey's journey, while the direct evidence of both Jérémie and La France seems so conclusive with regard to the other. La France indeed stated that Moose Lake (if this is "Lake Cariboux") runs northward "and then it spreads, and is wasted in a marshy Country, where there is no passing by Water, nor by Land in Summer." Hendry's purpose, 64 years after Kelsey's journey, and Cocking's also in 1772, was, of course, not only to bring the Indians to the Bay but to get them there by a route free from the French and Canadian posts on the Saskatchewan.

It is more difficult to reconcile Kelsey's departure for the prairie 28 miles up the Carrot River with the location of Deering's Point at Cedar Lake. In the *Journal* Kelsey estimates the distances travelled from Deering's Point as 18 miles the first day (July 15), 25 miles the next, 20 on July 17, and 8 on July 18 — 71 miles in all. If 28 of these were up the Carrot River, the distance from Cedar Lake to the mouth of the Carrot River would be only 43 miles by the winding Saskatchewan, whereas it would appear to be at least 50 miles as the crow files. Hendry, who reached the Saskatchewan in 1754 from Moose Lake at a point almost half way from Cedar Lake to the Carrot River, estimated his distance to Carrot River, as 8, 14, 6 and 16 miles — 44 miles in all. The total distance from Cedar Lake to the mouth of the Carrot River is estimated by Mr. Douglas, Secretary for the Geographic Board of Canada, at 71 miles.

Mr. Hugh Conn of the Hudson's Bay Company, whose first-hand knowledge of the northland is intimate and precise, has long held that Deering's Point was at the Pas, the only high and safe ground on the Saskatchewan in this neighbourhood. This too, however, is based upon the later data of the Moose Lake route rather than the more clearly contemporary evidence of Jérémie and La France.

Where geographers differ so widely no positive conclusion is, perhaps, possible. Will there ever be convincing direct evidence bearing upon Kelsey's route? When he left the stream on July 18, 1691, he took "ye Rundlett wch ye Governor had sent me full of powder & emptyed part of it into a leather Bagg so I put one hatchet 2 fathom of Black Tobacco 6 Knives 2 Skains of twine two nettlines one tin show [*sic*] & other small moveables into ye rundlett & headed it up again so we made a hole in the ground & put that & other things into it ... so made of it our storehouse untill we came yt way ye next spring." Next morning Kelsey "set forward into the woods." There is every likelihood that Kelsey came back during "ye next spring," for his "Rundlett," and for his canoe if nothing else; though abandoned canoes must have been no uncommon sight at this time on the Saskatchewan or Carrot Rivers. With birch bark, cedar, and watape one of these light canoes could be built in two or three days. But the "Rundlett" may never have been reclaimed. Will Kelsey's hatchet, 6 knives "and other small moveables" ever be found, like the La Vérendrye lead plate on the banks of the Missouri, to confirm or confound the theories of geographers and historians?

A modern artist's sketch of Henry Kelsey by H. Hatton, reproduced courtesy of the Saskatchewan Archives Board (R-D1818).

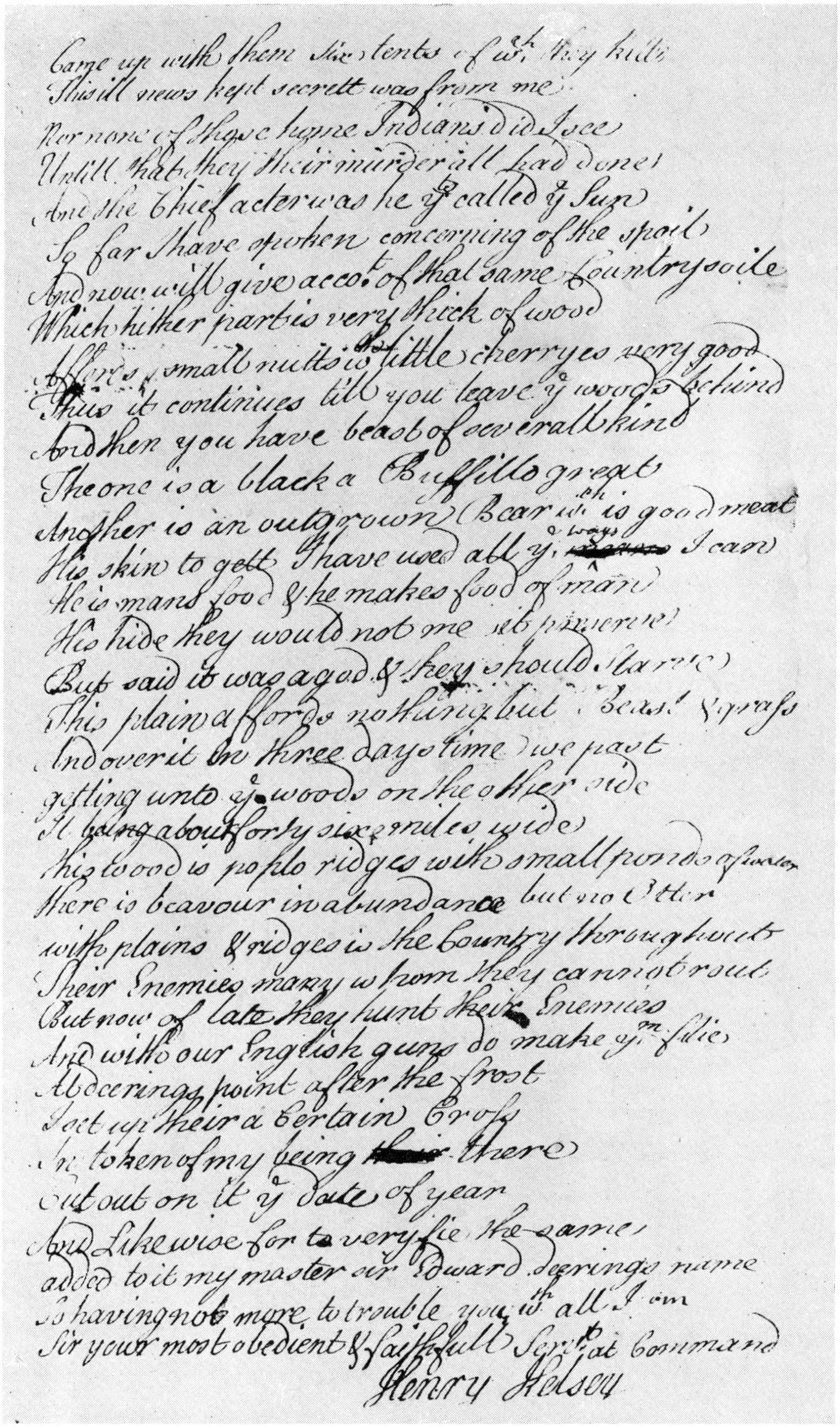
Came up with them Six tents of wch they kill'd
This ill news kept secrett was from me
Nor none of those home Indians did I see
Untill that they their murder all had done
And the Chief acter was he yt called ye Sun
So far I have spoken concerning of the spoil
And now will give accot of that same Country soile
Which hither part is very thick of wood
Affords small nutts wth little cherryes very good
Thus it continues till you leave ye woods behind
And then you have beast of severall kind
The one is a black a Buffillo great
Another is an outgrown Bear wch is good meat
His skin to gett I have used all ye ways I can
He is mans food & he makes food of man
His hide they would not me it preserve
But said it was a god & they should Starve
This plain affords nothing but Beast & grass
And over it in three days time we past
getting unto ye woods on the other side
It being about forty sixe miles wide
This wood is poplo ridges with small ponds of water
there is beavour in abundance but no Otter
with plains & ridges in the Country throughout
Their Enemies many whom they cannot rout
But now of late they hunt their Enemies
And with our English guns do make ym flie
At deerings point after the frost
I set up their a Certain Cross
In token of my being there
Cut out on it ye date of year
And Likewise for to veryfie the same
added to it my master sir Edward deerings name
So having not more to trouble you wth all I am
Sir your most obedient & faithfull Servt at Command
Henry Kelsey

Facsimile of page of original manuscript, in Kelsey's handwriting.

THE KELSEY PAPERS

Note

The text is based upon ***The Kelsey Papers*** *(Ottawa: King's Printer, 1929), and has been reproduced in as close an approximation to the original as was found possible. Occasionally in the manuscript a suprascript letter is separated from that below by a short line; these lines are omitted in the print. Letters or words which have been cancelled are here struck through; letters so blotted as to be illegible are indicated by asterisks. The slashes marking the ends of lines and pages in the 1929 edition have been eliminated here. The pagination numbers were added to the original by the Record Office of Northern Ireland, where the manuscript is housed, and are here enclosed in square brackets.*

Henry Kelsey his Book being ye Gift of James
Hubbud in the year of our Lord 1693

1690

Now Reader Read for I am well assur'd
Thou dost not know the hardships I endur'd
In this same desert where Ever y^{t} I have been
Nor wilt thou me believe without y^{t} thou had seen
The Emynent Dangers that did often me attend
But still I lived in hopes y^{t} once it would amend
And makes me free from hunger & from Cold
Likewise many other things wch I cannot here unfold
For many times I have often been oppresst
With fears & Cares y^{t} I could not take my rest
Because I was alone & no friend could find
And once y^{t} in my travels I was left behind
Which struck fear & terror into me
But still I was resolved this same Country for to see
Although through many dangers I did pass
Hoped still to undergo y^{m}, at the Last
Now Considering y^{t} it was my dismal fate
for to repent I thought it now to late
Trusting still unto my masters Consideration
Hoping they will Except of this my small Relation
Which here I have pend & still will Justifie
Concerning of those Indians & their Country
If this wont do farewell to all as I may say

[2]

And for my living i'll seek some other way
In sixteen hundred & ninety'th year
I set forth as plainly may appear
Through Gods assistance for to understand
The natives language & to see their land
And for my masters interest I did soon
Sett from y^{e} house y^{e} twealth of June
Then up y^{e} River I with heavy heart

Did take my way & from all English part
To live amongst y^{e}$_{\wedge}$^{Natives} of this place
If god permits me for one two years space
The Inland Country of Good report hath been
By Indians but by English yet not seen
Therefore I on my Journey did not stay
But making all y^{e} hast I could upon our way
Gott on y^{e} borders of y^{e} stone Indian Country
I took possession on ye tenth Instant July
And for my masters I speaking for y^{m}, all
This neck of land I deerings point did call
Distance from hence by Judgement at ye lest
From ye house six hundred miles southwest
Through Rivers wch run strong with falls
thirty three Carriages five lakes in all
The ground begins for to be dry with wood
Poplo & birch with ash thats very good
For the Natives of that place w^{ch}, knows
No use of Better than their wooden Bows
According to ye use & custom of this place
In September I brought those Natives to a peace
But I had no sooner from those Natives turnd my back
Some of the home Indians came upon their track
And for old grudges & their minds to fill

[3]

Came up with them Six tents of w^{ch}, they kill'd
This ill news kept secrett was from me
Nor none of those home Indians did I see
Untill that they their murder all had done
And the Chief acter was he y^{ts} called ye Sun
So far I have spoken concerning of the spoil
And now will give acco^{t}. of that same Country soile
Which hither part is very thick of wood
Affords small nuts wth little cherryes very good
Thus it continues till you leave y^{e} woods behind
And then you have beast of severall kind
The one is a black a Buffillo great
Another is an outgrown Bear w^{ch}, is good meat
His skin to gett I have used all y^{e}, ~~means~~$_{\wedge}$^{ways} I can
He is mans food & he makes food of man
His hide they would not me it preserve
But said it was a god & they should Starve
This plain affords nothing but Beast & grass
And over it in three days time we past
getting unto y^{e} woods on the other side
It being about forty sixe miles wide
This wood is poplo ridges with small ponds of water
there is beavour in abundance but no Otter
with plains & ridges in the Country throughout
Their Enemies many whom they cannot rout
But now of late they hunt their Enemies
And with our English guns do make y^{m}, flie

At deerings point after the frost
I set up their a Certain Cross
In token of my being ~~their~~ there
Cut out on it y^e date of year
And Likewise for to veryfie the same
added to it my master sir Edward deerings name
So having not[1] more to trouble you wth all I am
Sir your most obedient & faithfull $Serv^t$. at Command

HENRY KELSEY

1691

[4]

A Journal of a voyage & Journey undertaken
by henry Kelsey through Gods assistance
to discover & bring to a Commerce the
Naywatame poets in Anno 1691

July y^e 15th

Now having Receivd those things in full
wch y^e Governour sent me taketh my depart
from Deerings Point to seek for ye Stone
Indians wch were gone ten days before we having
but very little victuals paddled about 18 Miles
& Came too

July y^e 16th

Today setting forward again we went through
a little creek were we were forc'd to track
our Cannoes into an Island within wch is great
ponds of water & so padling from one to another
~~from one to another~~ $^{\text{sometimes running}}$ through long high grass
wch grows in near 2 foot water this grass hath
an Ear like our English Oats Distance today 25
Miles & came to in a small poplo Island

July y^e 17th

We put on our way again paddling still in y^e
same as before untill about 3 a Clock in y^e afternoon
& then coming to a Carriage near half a Mile
long wch came out at ye Riverside again ye Stream
Running very strong & having no Sustinence
Whereby to follow our Chase we concluded for
to take our Course into ye woods on ye morrow
having gott about 20 Miles today

July ye 18th

Today we paddled up ye Rivers untill about
noon & then we came to a small arm of y^e
River ~~side~~ so we concluded to sett our netts
& lay up our Cannoes & Rest ye remaining
part of the day there wch accordingly we did
so I took~~ed~~ ye Rundlett wch ye Governor had

[5]

sent me full of powder & emptyed part of it into a
leather Bagg so I put one hatchet 2 fathom of ~~Blag~~

---

1 The "t" has been partially deleted.

Black Tobacco 6 Knives 2 Skains of twine two nettlines one tin show & other small mov‸eables into ye rundlett & headed it up again so we made a hole in the ground & put that & other things into it & put into it so made of it our storehouse untill we came yt way ye next spring dist: 8 miles 3 pikes today

July ye 19th This morning we set forward into the woods & having travelled about 10 Miles pitcht a place for the tent & went out a hunting all Returning in the Evening having kill'd nothing but 2 wood pattridges & one Sq‸uirrell

July ye 20th So setting forward again we had not gone above 9 Miles but came on ye track of Indians wch we Judged had past four Days before so we went on till we came up with their old tents so we seeing they had kill two Beast I thought they might have had good store of victuals & not have been farr before us I sent an Indian before & fitted him out wth my pipe & some tobacco & bid him tell them to send me some relief & likewise for to stay for me this day we travelled about 18 Miles

July ye 21st This morning Setting forward again about 11 a Clock I met with yt same Indian wch I had sent away yesterday he telling me he had seen no Indians so I caused another hand to go away Immediately because I was so heavy Loaded my self yt I could not go having travelled to day near 16 Miles

July ye 22d This morning it Raind very hard but hunger forcing me to leave my Company I sett forward with 2 Indians to seek for those Indians wch were

[6]

gone before hopeing for to gett some relief of them by Estimation 25 Miles

July ye 23d Now about[Now about] noon one Indian return'd back fearing lest ye women would starve wch were behind so I gave him some powder & an Order to receive some shott of such a woman so I proceeded forward along wth a little slave Boy & toward night we came to good footing for all yt we had passed before was heavy mossy going so in the Evening wee came too dist 30 Mile & nothing to eat but one wood patridge

July ye 24th To day we had very good going & about noon we came up wth their tents they had left to day they having increas'd from 2 to 7 & their fire not being quite out we sat down & roasted 3 Pigeons wch I had kill'd yt morning & so went along again till about six in ye afternoon we came to their tents they having nothing but grass & Berryes to eat part of wch they gave to me but at night they're people returning from hunting one had kill'd 2 Swans & another had kill'd a Buck Muse but did not come home till in ye Night so I being asleep he sent his son to call me & when he came he told me y^{t} his father wanted me to come & smoke a pipe with him so I went & when I came he gave me a pipe to light & then presented me wth the great gut of ye Beast afore^{sd}, so when I had Eaten I returned to my rest having travelled to day 20 Miles

July ye 25th This morning I made a speech desireing y^{m} for to stay for our people wch was behind but an Old man came to me & told me y^{t} it would signify nothing for to lye still seeing y^{t} there was no victuals to Relieve y^{m} when they came up so desired leave of me to pitch a little way y^{t} ye women might fetch home ye Beast wch was kill'd ye day before y^{t} they might have wherewithall to relieve y^{m} when they came so I sent two women back for to help our women along wth their their things so we pitched about 10 Miles & came too

[7]

July ye 26th To day I bid y^{m} lie still & go a hunting wch accordingly they did & those wch was behind came up wth us in ye Evening our hunters Likewise coming hhome they having kill'd five Beast

July the 27th Now we pitcht ag ain & about 10 o Clock came to where one Beast lay to suffice our Hungry Bellyes & about 2 ~~o Clock five Indian strangers~~ in ye Afternoon their came five Indian strangers to our tents our Journey not Extending 7 Miles

July ye 28th This Instant ye Indians having told us their news wch was y^{t} they desired of us for to meet y^{m} at a place called Waskashreeseebee so I told y^{m} y^{t} we would make as much hast as we could Conveniently so in ye Evening the strangers returned to their tents we lying still this day & some of our men went a hunting

July ye 29th To day we pitched again having no want of victuals our hunters yesterday having kill'd some Beast to day our Journey not Extending 12 Miles

July ye 30th Now we pitched again about ten Miles & came to our Indians making a great feast telling y^{t} they were very glad y^{t} I was returned according to my promise for if I should be wanting they should be greatly afraid y^{t} ye Nayhaythaways Indians would murder y^{m} & so made me master of ye feast

July ye 31th This morning it Raind very hard so ye same Indian wch made ye feast last nigh presented

me wth 17 Beavour skins & it clearing up in y^{e}
afternoon we pitched about 9 Miles & came too

August ye 1st Wee pitched again & Gott to the River Afore^{sd}. where they appointed to meet us but they being gone before we followed their track we travelled to day about 15 Miles & came too

August ye 2^{d} Now we followed there track & in the Evening came up to y^{m} they being in number 26 tents & these Indians are called Eagles brich Indians our Journey not Extending 18 Miles

[8]

August ye 3^{d} So Being all together we pitched again by reason they had no great store of victuals went to day by Estimation 15 Miles

August ye 4th To day we lay still having strangers come to our tents from some stone Indians wch was to ye Southward of us so we made a tent for our strangers & provided them something to Eat & some Tobacco for to smoak it so they told us their news wch was y^{t} ye Nayhaythaways had lost 3 of their women wch ye Naywattame poets had killed‸^{ye} last spring & withall they appointed where they themselves would meet us but as for ye Naywattame poets they were fled so far y^{t} they thought I should not see them—

August ye 5th Now we pitched again our strangers Likewise Returning to their tents I telling y^{m} if by any means they could come to a speech of those Naywattame ~~poets~~ Indians for to give y^{m} all ye Encouragements Immaginable for to come to me & not to fear y^{t} any one should do y^{m} any harm so I gave two pieces of tobacco ye one for their guang ye other for ye Naywatame poet if they did see any of y^{m} our to day 12 Miles

August ye 6th To day we pitcht to y^{t} River wch I have spoken of before wch is not a hundred yards over & but very shoal water this River breants[1] away much to ye Southward & runneth through great part of the Cuntry & is fed by a lake wch feedeth another River wch runneth down to ye Southw ard of us and is called ~~Mith~~****
Now ye water wch runneth down this River is of a Blood red Colour by ye descripti on

[9]

---

1 Possibly "treants."

of those Indians wch hath seen it wch makes me to think y^{t} it may run through some mine or other our Journey this day by Estimation 10 Miles

August the 7th This Instant pitched up the side of this River afores^{d}. & in my Journey to day in Several places I Saw slate mines along the side of this River by ~~Estimation~~ dist; 10 Miles

August the 8th Now lying still I fitted out two Indians for to go see If they could find out ye mountain poets so if they found y^{m} for to tell y^{m} y^{t} I would meet y^{m} at a place wch was about 40 Miles a head of us & so they departed

August the 9th To day we pitched again still shaping our Course along the Riverside it Running or lying up between ye South South west but unnavigable for either boat or Cannoe ye Extent of our Journey not Exceeding 16 Miles

August the 10th We pitcht again ye Indians having kill'd great store of Beast ~~today~~ yesterday so where they lay thickest we came too dist: 8 Miles

August the 11th This day we lay still for the women to fetch home ye meat & Dress it ye Indians Likewise feasting & making of feasts all ye day

August ye 12th Now we pitcht again & about noon ye ground begins to grow ~~barren~~ heathy & barren in fields of about half a Mile over Just as if they had been Artificially made with fine groves of Poplo growing round y^{m} we went to day by Estimation 10 Miles

August ye 13th It Raining very hard caused us to lye still to day

August ye 14th This day we pitched again ye Ground Continuing as before But no fir growing the wood being for ye most part poplo & Birch having travelled to day 12 Miles came too

[10]

August ye 15th This Instant one Indian Lying a dying & withall a murmuring wch was amongst the Indians Because I would not agree for y^{m} to go to warrs so I taking it into Consideration cut some tobacco & call'd all ye Old dons to my tent telling y^{m} y^{t} it was not ye way for y^{m} to have the use of English guns & other things & y^{t} I nor they should not go near ye Govern^{r}. unless they ceast from warring so lay still to day

August ye 16th Now not knowing wch would Conquer life or Death lay still to day our people going a hunting but had small success

August y^{e} 17th Last night death ceased & this morning his body was burned according to their way they making A great feast for him y^{t} did it now after y^{t} y^{e} flesh was burned his Bones were taken & buried wth Loggs set up rou$_{\wedge}^{n}$d of about ten foot Long so we pitcht to day near 14 Miles & came to they holding it not good to stay by y^{e} Dead

August y^{e} 18th This day I sent two Indians for to seek for those wch I had sent before to see for y^{e} Mountain poets fearing lest they should have come to any damage being so long absent so we pitched ye ground Continuing as formerly dist 8 Miles

August ye 19th Now we sett forward again y^{e} ground being more Barren then it use to be y^{e} Indians having seen great store of Buffillo But kill'd none by Estimat ion 12 Miles

August y^{e} 20th To day we pitcht to y^{e} outtermost Edge of y^{e} woods this plain affords Nothing but short Round sticky grass & Buffillo & a great ~~sor~~$_{\wedge}^{sort}$ of a Bear wch is Bigger then any white Bear & is Neither White nor Black But silver hair'd like our English Rabbit y^{e} Buffillo Likewise is not like those to y^{e} Northward their Horns growing like an English Ox but Black & short dist: 6 Miles

[11]

August y^{e} 21st This day we lay Expecting a post from ye mountaine poets but none came

August ye 22^{d} Now we pitched into the barren ground it being very dry heathy land & no water but here & there a small pond so we came to but could not see ye woods on ye other side dist 16 Miles

August ye 23^{d} This Instant ye Indians going a hunting Kill'd great store of Buffillo Now ye manner of their hunting these Beast on ye Barren ground is when they see a great parcel of them together they surround them wth men wch done they gather themselves into a smaller Compass Keeping ye Beast still in ye middle & so shooting y^{m} till they break out at some place or other & so gett away from y^{m} our women Likewise pitching according to order dist 12 Miles

August ye 24th This day lay still waiting for a post wch came in ye afternoon from ye Capt: of the Mountain Poets Named Washa so ye Substance of their news was y^{t} he desired we would meet him when we pitcht again so I told y^{m} I would

August ye 25 ^{S}So pitching again we came to altogether & in number we were 80 Tents we having travelled to day by Estimation 12 Miles yet not reacht ye woods on ye other side this plain running through great part of ye Country & lyeth along near East & west

August ye 26 Now we are altogether they made a feast ye which they Invited me to so they desired leave of me for y^{m} to go to wars but

I told y^m y^t I could not grant y^m their request for ye Govern^r. would not allow me so to do so we lay still to day

August ye 27th To day we pitched again & got to ye woods on ye other side ye Plain being about 46 miles over our Journey not Extending 6 miles /

August ye 28th This day we lay still ye Indians being willing for to go hunt Buffillo because there is none of these Beast in ye woods so I condescended to it so I called six Indians & fitted y^m out wth tobacco & powder & shott & bid y^m go seek for some Naywatame poets & if so be y^t they found y^m I would Reward y^m sufficiently

[12]

August ye 29th This Instant we lay still for ye women to fetch home Meat & dress it our Indians Likewise going a Beavour hunting for in these woods there is abundance of small ponds of water of which there is hardly one Escapes without a Beavour house or two our people having kill'd great store to day

August ye 30th Now we pitched again directing our Course into the woods it being all poplo & birch & high Champion land wth ponds as afore^{sd}. our Indians dispercing themselves some ahunt ing of beast & some of beavour Dist 8 Miles

August ye 31st This day ye Indians made a feast desireing of me to be a post to a parcel of Indians wch was to ye Northward of us to desire y^m to stay for us telling me y^t my word would be taken before an Indians although he went so we lay still to day

September ye 1st Now being in their Enemies Country I had eight Indians for my conduct one of wch Could speak both Languages for to be my interpreter so set forward & having travelled to day near 30 miles in ye Evening came to in a small poplo Island wch standeth out from ye main Ridge of woods because these Indians are greatly afraid of their Enemies

Septr. ye 2^d This morning Setting forward again it Proved very bad weather & by reason of so many beaten paths wch ye Buffillo makes we lost ye track so I filled two pipes of Tobacco according to their way so I speaking to two young men to go seek for ye track & when I ~~h**~~ had Ended my speech I gave Each of y^m a pipe to light so they departed & it being cold we made a fire but a great parcel of Buffillo appearing in sight we gave y^m Chase & by ye way found ye track & in ye Eveni ng came up wth y^m we travelled to day by Estimation 25 Miles

September ye 3^d This morning they provided a feast for me to hear w^t I had to say so told y^m, my message wch was to stay for those wch I came from now I understanding their drift was to come altogether for to go to wars so I told y^m y^t they must not go to wars for it will not be liked by ye governer neither would he trade with y^m if they did not cease from warring

[13]

Septr. the 4th To day I sent two Indians back for to tell our people for to make w^{t} hast they could to me I tarrying ~~for to~~ there my self for to hear w^{t} News some ~~some~~ young men brought wch went from thence three days before I came for to look for their Enemies

Septr. the 5th About ten o Clock this morning ye young men appearing in sight & crying out‸^{Just}like a Crane wch gave a sign y^{t} they had discovered their Enemies & as soon as they came within one hundred yards of ye tent they ~~Enem~~sat all down in a Row upon the grass not speaking one word so ye old Men lighting their pipes went to y^{m} & served y^{m} round Crying as if they had been stob'd for Joy they had found their enemies ye young men having brought some old arrows to verifie w^{t} they had been about

Septr. ye 6th This Instant I unclosed ye pipe wch ye governour had sent me telling y^{m} y^{t} they must Imploy their time in Catching of beav our for y^{t} will be better liked on then their killing their Enem ies when they come to ye factory neither was I sent there for to kill any Indians but to make peace wth as many as I could but all my arguments prevailed nothing wth y^{m} for they told me w^{t} signified a piece wth those Indians considering they knew not ye use of Cannoes & were resolved to go to wars so I seeing it in vain I held my peace

Septr. ye 7th This day we pitcht again & got through ye woods this ledge not being above 30 Miles through but we made it a great deal more by reason we kept in it for to hunt beavour & to come altogether this plain being in ye same Nature of ye other wch we had past before our Journey not Extending 10 Miles

Septr. ye 8th Now likewise we pitched again & by ye way met wth those Indians wch I came post from & so came too altogether this afternoon came four Indian strangers from those wch are called Naywatame po‸^{e}ts ye wch I receiv'd very kindly & made much of y^{m} Likewise our own people returning wth y^{m} so I inquired where there Capt was they giving me an acco^{t}. y^{t} he was two days Journey behind our Journey to day not Extending 8 Miles

Septr. ye 9th This morning I went to ye Capt. of ye stone Indians tent carry ing wth me a piece of tobacco I telling him to make a speech to all his Country men & tell y^{m} not to disturbe nor meddle wth ye Naywattame poets for I was going back to Invite & incourage y^{m} to a peace once more so they all gave their Consent & told me y^{t} they were very free to have y^{m} to be their friends so I took my way back along wth those wch came yesterday having 12 tents along wth me our Journey to day 18 Miles

[14]

Septr. ye 10th This day setting out again my strangers told me they would go before & give an acco^{t} y^{t} I was coming because they could make better way to their tents then I could so we travell'd till night & came to dist 20 Miles

Septr. ye 11th

Now setting forward again about noon came up wth their track & in ye Evening came too altogether they being in number 11 tents our Journey not Extending 16 Miles

Septr. ye 12th

This morning having no victuals to invite ye cap^t. to so I filled y^t pipe wch ye Govern^r. had sent me wth tobacco & then sent for ye Capt. So then I made a speech to him & told him y^t he should not mind w^t had passed formerly as concerning ye nayhaythaways killing Six tents of his Country men & for ye future we English will seek for to prevent it going any further for if so be they did so any more ye Govern^r. says he will not trade wth y^m if they did not cease from killing his friends & when I had done I presented him wth a present coat & sash Cup & one of my guns wth knives awls & tobacco wth small quantities of powder & shott & part of all such things as ye Govern^r. had sent me so he seemed to be very well pleased & told me he had forgott w^t had past although they had kill'd most of his kindred & relations & likewise told me he was sorry he had not wherewithall for to make me Restitution for w^t I had given him but he would meet me at Deerings point ye next spring & go wth me to ye factory but it happened in the winter after I had parted wth them ye Nayhaythaways came up wth y^m & killed two of y^m wch struck a new fear into y^m y^t they would not venture down fearing lest ye home Indians would not let y^m up again into their own Country so when I was at Deerings point in the spring wch is ye place of resortance when they are coming down to trade upon ye arrival of some indians I had news brought me y^t y^e ~~****~~ ^Capt.^{r}. afores^d. had sent me a pipe & steam of his own making & withall ye news of their being kill'd as I have spoken of before yet if so be I would send him a piece of tobacco from ye factory upon ye return of ye same indians he would certainly come down ye next year But if not ye beavour in their Cuntry are unnumerable & will certainly be brought down every year so having not to inlarge sir I remain your obedient & faithfull Servt.

HENRY KELSEY

[15]

1691 - 1692

Now I shall according to ye best of my knowledge give an Acco^t. of those Indians belief & Superstitions in their ways & how they make use of them ———
Their first & Chiefest point is A piece of Birch rine full of Feathers of Divers sorts put on a piece of Leather wch is broad at one End for to tie about their head at such a sort y^t ye remaining part shall hang down over their back this they put to use when their Enemies are in sight believing y^t it will save y^m from being kill'd, It being not ye work of their own hands But of their father or some other old man near kin to y^m This thing is called by their name Wessguaniconan wch in time of use is accompanied wth songs made by y^e

same man wch made ye other wch songs are Called Wonny seewahiggens so much for the first point

Their second point is Concerning A pipe steam done wth feathers of Divers sorts & near y^{t} end wch goeth into ye mouth is three voulter or Eagles feathers split & lay'd on like ye feathers of an arrow Now every one of these & all things Else belonging to the steam Afore^{sd}. hath a speech belongs to every one of y^{m} as ye makers fancy leads him Now there is but very few Indians but w^{t} are beading Indians y^{t} can get one of these pipes & when he hath a mind to go to warrs or any other way he calls all of y^{m} together & tells y^{m} his mind so then he Lights his pipe & serveth y^{m} Round Crying Now their Custom is to take but four Whiffs of those pipes & if any one hath not a mind to go wth him nor answer his request he will Likewise refuse to smoke out of his pipe & again if any man hath made use of a woman ye last night or his wife be wth Child he will pass by the pipe & give thanks if he has a Mind to go wth him for they think they shall adulter ate ye pipe if they should smoke out of it at such a time Likewise they will send these pipes out upon any expedition as when they go for to seek out their Enemies tracks or when y^{t} they are in want of victuals they will fitt a young man out wth a pipe steam & if it happens y^{t} it fulfills w^{t} they design then it doth pass for a true god Ever afterwards although it hath been never so false before

[16]

The next point being their third is when they are in want of any thing but victuals especially in ye night they will cause ye tent to be made Close & ye fire to thrown out of doors Likewise ye women must be absent so all things being dark & husht one of ye Indians will begin to make a speech wch Endeded he will fall a singing till such time he thinks he has pleasured ye Company & then will begin for to Whistle Making his fellows believe y^{t} he hath a familiar they believing it to be so to so by y^{t} means he will answer y^{m} to any ques tion they shall ask him & will tell y^{m} wch way they ~~sha~~ shall go to look for victuals or to find other india^{ns} & this ye Natives holds for truth but I have found it often to be lyes

Now their fourth point is if any of y^{m} be sick they use no other means nor know no other help but to sing to ye sick for wch purpose they hire a man & he calls together some men more or less for to accompa nie him in his singing so all of y^{m} getting a piece of birch Rine & a little stick goes to the sick mans tent then he y^{ts} hired begins to sing & ye Rest Beats upon ye Rine ye same stroke he uses wth his rattle wch is made of Birch rine hallow within having some stones or

Beads Inclosed in it so when he has sat & sung a
while to his patient he y^{ts} hired will rise up stark
naked making a hideous noise & having there
ready a Dish of Cold water takes a mouthfull
of it & spurts on ye sick person so following
it Close wth his mouth sucks at his skin &
Rising from him again halls drugs or something
out of his mouth so makes his fellows believe he
suckt it out of ye sick person, & indeed is hard to be
perceiv'd to ye Contrary Now in such times they
will take ye best things they have & hang upon

[17]

Poles as an offering to him wch was ye cause of his sickness
Likewise making along speech desiring of him to send him
his health again Now as for a woman they do not so much
mind her for they reckon she is like a Slead dog or
Bitch when she is living & when she dies they think
she dyes to Eternity but aman they think departs
into another world & lives again
Then their fifth point is this If at any time they are
in want of victuals they will fitt a young man out wth
something of their own making as it may be half a
dozen peruant stones wch they have gott from ye factory
or Else a pipe steam now these pruant stones they
scrape smooth & burn spots, or ye shape of any thing
as their fancy leads y^{m} now if happens y^{t} this young man
wch is fitted out should kill a Beast y^{t} day then they
will impute it to ye things he carried about him &
so it passes for a God Ever afterwards But now no
Beast they kill but some part or other is allotted
for mans meat wch ye women are not to tast of upon no
acco^{t}, but more especialy at this time then others by
reason they think it will be a hindrance to their
Killing any more Beast nay if a woman should eat
any of this mans mans meat wch is called in their Langu
age ~~Crett**tgh~~ Cuttawatchetaugun & fall sick in a
year or 2 afterwards & dye they will not stick to say
it was y^{t} kill'd her for all it was so long ago she eat it
Their sixth point I shall relate is concerning
their singing of their songs & from whence they think
they have y^{m} those that they reckon Chiefly for gods are
Beast & fowl But of all Beast ye Buffillo & of all fowls
ye voulter & ye Eagle wch they say they dream of in their
sleep & it relates to y^{m} w^{t} they shall say when they sing
& By y^{t} means whatsoever they ask or require will be gran
ted or given y^{m} wch by often making use of it sometimes happe
ns to fall out Right as they say & for y^{t} one time it will
pass for a truth y^{t} he hath a familliar although he
hath told never so many lies before & so by their

[18]

singing will pretend to know ^^{wt} y^{e} firmament of heaven is ~~m~~
made of nay some Indians wch I have discoursed wth has told me they

have been there & seen it so likewise another has told me y^{t} he
had been so near$_{\wedge}^{to}$ y^{e} sun at y^{e} going down y^{t} he ~~had been so~~ could
take hold of it when it Cut y^{e} Horrizon Likewise they would
pretend to tell me by their singing how things stood at y^{e}
factory when I was many hundred miles of along wth y^{m} but
I found it not true ————————
Now there is a Difference between ye stone Indians & y^{e}
Nayhaythaways although ye principles of their belief is
all one & ye same But I mean as to passages in their tents
wch I shall give some small relation of I having been amongst
ye stone Indians of late will begin wth y^{m} first Now if they
have a mind for to make a feast they will pitch a tent
on purpose & after y^{t} ye tent is made & fixt then no woman
Kind y^{t} hath a husband or is known to have been concern'd
wth a man must not come within the door of ye tent afore^{sd}.
so then ye master of ye tent & one or two more goeth in & Cutteth
out a place for ye fire about three foot square in ye middle
of ye tent & then ye fire being made they take a little
sweet grass & lay at every corner of ye said square &
then putting fire to it they perfume the tent so
making along speech wishing all health &
happiness both to founders & confounders this
being done ye master burning a little more sweet
grass then taketh a pipe fill'd wth tobacco & perfum
eth it so giveth it to another Indian telling him
who he shall call to ye feast so then he goeth
out of doors & those wch are appointed he calls by name
two or 3 times over & then returning into ye tent
again lights the pipe wch was given him ye pipe being
lighted he turneth y^{t} end wch goeth into ye mouth
to w^{t} place ye master of ye feast shall direct him w^{ch}
generally first towards our English house & from
thence moving it round gradually towards ye sun
rising & so about to ~~****~~ where ye sun is at noon
still keeping in motion to where ye sun goeth down
& then turneth y^{t} end wch goeth into ye mouth toward
ye ground so lighting it ye second time handeth it
round to his companions & as they receive it they

[19]

give thanks so when they are all gathered together
ye master will have some victuals & some tobacco ready
cut wth wch they will sing & be merry as we do over a Cup
of good liquor now they have but two or three Words in
a song & they observe to keep time along wth him y^{t} is
ye leader of ye song for Every man maketh his own songs
by vertue of w^{t} he dreams of as I have said before &
at ye Conclusion of every song they give thanks all
in general to him y^{t} ye song belongs too So likewise if
any one hath crost or vext them y^{t} they owe him
any grudge they will pretend to set w^{t} they dream
of to work & it shall kill the offender at his pleasure

Torn out[1]

nor step over a man boy nor Child for if at any time
they should happen to stride over any one & y^{e}
person fall sick at any time after they will impute
it to be ye reason of it & likewise when they are
sick they will call themselves to remembrance
to see if y^{t} they have eat any thing wch has been forbid
den y^{m} to eat & if it happened by force of hunger
they have eat w^{t} has been forbidden y^{m} then presently
y^{t} is ye cause of their sickness & if they should dye
y^{t} fitt they still think that is the cause of it

1689

A Journal of a voyage & Journey undertaken
by Henry Kelsey to discover & Endeavour to bring
to a Commerce ye nothern Indians Inhabiting to y^{e}
Northward of Churchill River & also ye dog[2]side Nation

June ye 17th 1689

June ye 17th Munday 1689 I took my depart^{r}. from Churchill River in ye Hopewell
shallop Commanded by Capt: James young & my Companion
wch was appointed by my Governor ye wind being at south

Torn out till the 26th

Leagues before we was forc'd ashore by ye Ice now
we Judged our selves to be about 20 Leagues from
Churchill River

ye 26 Munday This morning ye Ice being nearer than before I told
ye Capt. y^{t} ye tediousness of getting along shore wth y^{e}
boat troubled me & I thought I could make better
way by land so desired ~~leave~~ ye Capt. to let me go

[20]

wch he Consented I should sett forward on ye morrow upon
this gave me my Instructions wch he had from my ~~Govern^{r}~~
Govern^{r}. at Hays river

June ye 27th Tuesday This day by gods assistance set forward by land so
desired Capt. young to let 2 of his hands go to carry some
things till I could hide y^{m} because we carry y^{m} all accord
ingly they did this done we parted & in our Journey we
found five targets Made of Boards six Inches wide
& Sowed together till they were about 2 foot over & then
cut round like ye head of a Cask so wth a string in ye middle
to hang over their arm distance 12 Miles to day

ye 28th Wednesday This morning set forward but my dog run back to

---

1 This and other similar entries are in the original hand.
2 Possibly "y".

cap^{t}. youngs tent so bid my Companion stay till I went back to fetch him when I came I left y^{t} & took ye other wch my Governour had appointed me & when I was at ye tent Satisfied ye Capt. concerning ye smoke we made ye day before because it was to be a sign we found a River so returned to my Companion

y^{e} 29th Thursday This days Journey most part ponds & hills we being near 8 Miles from y^{e} seaside about ten o'Clock found an old Cannoe of those northern Indians abundance of Musketers & at night could not gett wood Enough for to make a smoke to Clear y^{m} came to dist ~~13 Miles~~$_{\wedge}$$^{23\ Miles\ no}$woods in sig^{sight}

y^{e} 30th friday To day we travelled all within Land it being all hills & more barren then before y^{e} hills being all stones wth a coat of moss over y^{m} came to dist 18 Miles

July y^{e} 1st Saturday This morning set forward it being hills & ponds wch would put us out of our way 2 or 3 Miles although we went good days Journey it did not seem so dist 18 Miles

ye 2^{d} Sunday The same going as before at noon it Raind hard having no shelter but ye heavens for a Cannope nor^{nor} no wood to make a fire came dist 12 Miles

ye 3^{d} Monday This day setting forward more hilly then before & more Rocky ~~than before~~ came to one[1] ye top of one where we could see ye sea dist 16 Mile & from ye sea 6 Miles

ye 4th Tuesday To day set forward till about noon it Raind very hard caused us to come to dist 8 Miles

[21]

ye 5th Wednesday Now we intended to go to ye sea side for better going but found ye same & foggy by reason of ye Ice toward night came to ye Boy not suffering me to speak aloud in pretence ye Eskemoes would hear us dist 16 Miles

ye 6th Thursday To day continued foggy & Could not gett my Companion to go further wch was ye first I perceived of his backward ness so came to dist 5 Mile

ye 7th friday To day had very good going till about noon coming to an outlet & trying to get over at several places but could not so tarryed there ye night dist 10 Miles

ye 8th Saturday This morning got over ye River 3 Mile up this River is a high round hummock being ye best landmark we have seen

ye 9th sunday Setting forward good weather & going as it were on a Bowling green in ye Evening spyed two Buffillo left our things & pursued y^{m} we Kill'd one they are ill

---

1 The "e" is partially erased.

shapen beast their Body being bigger than an ox leg & foot like ye same but not half so long a long neck & head a hog their Horns not growing like other Beast but Joyn together upon their forehead & so come down ye side of their head & turn up till ye tips be Even wth ye Buts their Hair is near a foot long this being ye first Killing of Beast since we left Capt. young so went back to our things our Journey not Extending 10 Miles

July ye 10th Munday To day carried our things to where ye Beast lay & to argue why he would go no further he answer'd ye Summer was to far spent & y^{t} his Country people was gone to far to ye northward for fear of ye southern Indians y^{t} it would be hard finding of y^{m} but if y^{t} Capt. young could have carryed him to y^{t} River wch they call Buffillo River he did not question finding of y^{m} dist 3 Mile

ye 11th Tuesday This day through many perswasions gott him to go ten Miles & then he told me I was a fool & y^{t} he ~~woul~~ would go no further for I was not sensable of ye dangers we had to go through so came to dist 10 Miles

ye 12 Wednesday This morning he told me he would go no further so I thought it needless to spend my time in vain resolv'd to make ye best of my way to Churchill River to give a[1] acco^{t}. of it & to do something more servicable for m[2] Masters so Returned back dist: 21 Miles

[22]

ye 13th Thursday This day finding our Burdens heavy concluded to leave some things for a mark so left 1 Bottle of Powder & some shott 2 Ice Chizzels 4 hatchets on ye top of a flatt stone so setting forward saw two Buffillo & kill'd one dist 17 Miles

ye 14th Friday To day we had level going till four in ye afternoon it began to grow hilly & Rain'd very hard so came to & made a tent of moss dist 19 Miles

ye 15th Saturday It Rained hard most part of ye day yet travelled ye Hills trent to ye sea side & makes it bold to for it flowes 5 fathom steep up & down dist 17[3] Miles

ye 16th Sunday Now setting forward we found it hilly & more barren then within land dist 22 Miles

ye 17th Monday To day at noon Came to for to kill deer my partner kill'd five & I four dist 18 Miles

---

1 End of paper frayed.
2 Ibid.
3 Figures uncertain; perhaps 15.

ye 18th Tuesday

This day we gott to ye place where cap^t. young put us ashore at four this afternoon broke open our store house & went to carry ye things over ye River having made a Raft of all ye wood we could gett but it would not Carry us & the ~~things~~ goods so put ye Boy & things on it & swim'd over it my my self being very cold came to dist 24 Miles

ye 19th Wednesday

To day ye woods appear in sight about ten o Clock it Rain'd hard wth thunder & Lightening so we came to being ye first place of shelter we had found since we left Capt. young dist 5 Miles

July ye 20th Thursday

This day very bad going on great pibble stones wth great ponds ~~of water~~ three or four Mile over toward evening good going came too dist 14 Miles

ye 21st friday

This morning had very good going on hard mud wth great stones at three this afternoon came too an outlett & came too dist 16 Miles

ye 22^d Saturday

This morning tryed to gett over ye mouth of it but could not so left our things there & went up ye river to Raft our selves over & to fetch y^m wth a Boat from Churchill River so finding a good place of wood came too dist 15 Miles

[23]

the 23^d Sunday

To day it Rain'd hard & we had forgott our lines so I went to fetch y^m & Returned to him in ye Evening

ye 24th Munday

This morning made a Raft & got over to an Island wch we thought had been ye south shore but had not gone a Mile before we came to another Channel wch seemed to be worse then ye first so made a Raft against next morning

ye 25th Tuesday

To day put from‸ ^{ye} shore it being dreadfull to behold ye falls we had to pass Considering we had nothing to tye our Raft but small Logline & were forct to shoot 3 Desperate falls ye Raft struck upon two of y^m but gott safely over dist ¾ of a Mile

ye 26th Wednesday

Now setting forward went by ye hummock wch Capt. Young was speaking of wch stands on ye south side of ye River travelled to day till we raised ye high land of Churchill river & ye woods being Near ye water side came too dist 20 Miles

ye 27th Thursday

This morning went on our way but meeting wth many small creeks hindred us greatly at tide time gott to day 9 Mile

ye 28th Friday

To day at noon being upon ye high rocks of Chur chill River saw ye ship so went against her & made a smoke but it being low water they could not come to me so they put one hand ashore who told me there was a house a Building & at tide time went on board wth him dist 14 Miles

ye 29th Saturday To day I Rested on Board

ye 30th Sunday This day I went up wth a Boat to ye house & thomas savage told me y^{t} ye Governer had order'd me to tarry there wch I Refused by Reason I had a mind to go for England I spoke to Thomas savage Concerning those things wch I had left & desired him to speak to some to go wth me to fetch y^{m} but he answered he would not so I asked who would go so Edwd. Pratt Edwd. Bull Isaac hubbud Ely gramer & Thos. Harris would go wth me

July ye 31st Munday This noon tide we set from ye ship to fetch ye things so Rowed & sailed all night ye wind being between ye south & ye East

[24]

August ye 1st Tuesday This morning att day saw ye hummock about two Leagues from us so getting to ye place where ye things could not find a place to leave ye Boat while we fetcht y^{m} but was forct to ride her of wth one hand till we fetcht y^{m} so put y^{m} in ye Boat & put away but had not gott three Leagues ~~£**~~ before it Blow'd hard & Night coming on put ashore seeing some Deer I kill'd one & fetcht it to ye tent this Evening

ye 2^{d} Wednesday To day ye weather Continuing ye same we put away & Rowed to windward all day & at night came to anchor near ye shore wth ye high Land of Churchill River in sight

ye 3^{d} Thursday This day Rowed across ye Bay & saved ye afternoon tide to ye ship & ye first news we heard was y^{t} ye house was Reduced to ashes & y^{t} most of ye things were Burnt so I took my things & put y^{m} in my Chest

ye 4th Friday This day ye rest of ye things were fetcht on board from ye house

ye 5th Saturday This day broke ground from Churchill River Intending by gods assistance for Hays River ye wind being at North Turn it out & sailed all night

ye 6th Sunday This morning left of Raining & came on foggy & we saw breakers both within & without us but Edging towards ye outtermost gott clear & in ye afternoon came to anchor in ye mouth of Portnelson & Rid ye night

ye 7th Munday To day ye wind dullered & at tide time stood for Hayes River & at Night came to anchor in ye mouth of it

ye 8th Tuesday To day got to ye house & as soon as I could get a shore I went to ye Govern^{r}. taking ye Indian Boy

wth me & acquainted him how I had been serv'd by
him ye Governors reply was y^{t} I had my labour
for my travell since y^{t} ye Govern^{r}. Never did Require
any further acco^{t}. of me

HENRY KELSEY

[25]

1694

York fort hayes River August ye 8th 1694

Mr Smith

This is to satisfie you y^{t} we are safe arived praised be
god for it I understand ye albemarle was sent for
Churchill river but meeting wth much ice was drove
to ye southward of this place had like to have been lost
but by providence was saved arrived some small time
before us as for other things all is very well & a good trade
ye wch I hope will continue likewise hoping your
honour will not forgett him who hath Endeavour'd
for it Thos. Hart hath been guilty of a private
trade wch you will have a larger acco^{t}. from y^{e} ~~gover~~
govern^{r}. & as for my own part I shall neither do nor
act on any discovery untill I receive further
orders from my masters in England then shall be
very free to use ye utmost endeavours for as much
as I find no alterations yet but shall be more
able to give you a larger Epistle ye next Return
hoping to receive a line or two from your honour
by ye next as for my keeping a Journal I cannot by
Reason I am lik‸^{e}ly to abroad as much as at home so
having not to inlarge I Rest

your obedient & ~~fath~~
faithfull Servt.

HENRY KELSEY

If you please to inquire of y^{e}
Bearer he can better Inform
you of anything than I can at present

[26]

1696

Memmorandum in ye hudsons bay frigatt

June ye 2^{d} 1696 Being tuesday we weigh'd from gravesend & fell down
to ye lower end of ye hope & came to anchor

June ye 7th Sunday Weigh'd from ye lower end of ye hope & about 7 in ye Evening
going by ye man of war Rideing at ye nore having
taken in our pendants & lower'd our topsailes he
fired six guns at us & sent his boat on board cap^{t}.
Bayley to dem^{d}. money for his shot so in ye mouth

of ye swin came to anchor Capt. Bayley Sent his Boat to fetch M^{r}. Man wch ye man of wars boat had carryed away wth y^{m} it Blowing very hard ye deerings Boat could not gett aboard again

June ye 8th Munday Our Boat went aboard ye man of war to gett news of ye Deerings Boat ye ships weighed Likewise & bore up to ye man of war till high water so turn'd to windward seeing ye Deerings Boat coming of shore & about half tide came a ground on us[1] and called ye mouse at 11 att night being a quarter flood gott into ye Channel & came to anchor

June ye 9th Tuesday This morning set saile & in ye Evening came to ye Men of war at albourough so came to anchor

June ye 13th Saturday This afternoon sailed from alborough & in ye Evening came to ye other Man of war of Lastaf & came to anchor

June ye 14th Sunday About four this morning weighed again & in ye afternoon came to anchor in ye offing to ye northward about an hours time

June ye 15th Munday This day ye Commodore gave our Capt. Instructions for making of signes

June ye 16th Tuesday This day it Blowed hard we saw two saile but did not speak wth y^{m}

June ye 17th Wednesday This morning saw two sail & in ye afternoon one sail more to wch ye seaford gave Chase but soon left of & in ye Evening saw ye land of aberdeen

[27]

June ye 18th Thursday This morning stood Close to ye land ye fishing boats came of to us of we bought some parcels of fish sm[2] brease of wind stood of & on all day here came a master of a new England Briggantine who told us he was chast in there by three french privateers two of ~~abo~~ about 30 guns ye other a small vessell

June y^{e} ~~18th~~ 19th ~~Thursday~~ friday This morning was of Backeness & about noon our 3 Cap^{ts}. met on board y^{e} Deering & in y^{e} Evening came aboard again

June y^{e} 20th Saturday To day Capt. Bayley Invited all y^{e} Command^{rs}. aboard to dinner where they remained till Evening calm wth small breezes this two days past

June y^{e} 21st Sunday This morning was of Canards head wth small bre$_{\wedge}^{e}$zes of wind att North & N N W till Evening &

---

1 Appears to be an "a"corrected to "u".

2 Edge of paper frayed.

	then came up a fresh gale northerly we reeft three topsails
June ye 22d Munday	To day y^e Deering left of towing y^e knight & y^e Bonadventure took her in a tow y^e Deering Likewise unbent their main topsail foresaile & foretopsail & brought others too ye yards it continued northerly wind a Moderate gale
June ye 23d Tuesday	This morning A little wind northerly we stood into ye firth Close under an Island called sweatah where we turned to & fro to spend ye flood
June ye 24th Wednesday	This morning turned away for[1] S^t. Margarets hope & about six o Clock ye Bon[2]adventure came aground & lay till 10 ye fore[3]noon young flood gott of & sent hasser aboard of us & heaved into deep water so rid all night
June ye 25th Thursday	This morning weigh'd & stood for Caston proving calm gott not there till ye afternoon tide
June ye 26th friday	To day our ships watered & in ye Evening ye wind came up southerly
June ye 27th Saturday	About 4 this morning weighed from Caston & just out of hoyhead ye pilot went ashore ye wind at S S W about noon ye wind veared forward in y^e
	[28]
	Afternoon ye Bonadventure took us in a tow & ye seaford took ye knight in a tow towards night a fresh gale at W S W Reeft topsailes & handed main topsailes & mizzen topsailes & 12 at night saw a s[4] saile bearing down upon us after making w^t we was went away before ye wind
June ye 28th Sunday	To day it Blew hard put us by our topsail ye wind at W b S & W S W about two this afternoon our tow rope broke & at four ye knights broke also so ye men of war wen wth an Easy sail
June ye 29th Munday	This day it continued a fresh gale this afternoon ye Deering bore away & took ye knight in tow having as much wind as could carry our topsails
June ye 30th Tuesday	This afternoon it blowing very hard ye knight broak her tow handed our topsails & at 12 M N Lay a try

---

1 Read by piecing together some loose scraps of paper.
2 Ibid.
3 Ibid.
4 Partially erased.

July ye 1st Wednesd This morning bore away to ye knight & about
two this afternoon set our foresaile ye wind being
at W b N & W N W a hard gale

July ye 2^{d} Thursday This morning ~~bore away to ye Knight~~‸ four o Clock ye wind dullered we set out
topsailes & about ten ye bonadventure bore away &
took y^{e}[1] knight in a tow about 3 this afternoon
came down in a[2] squall in wch ye deering lost her foretop
mast & mizzen[3] top mast so we Reeft our topsails
& bore down to him & askt him if he wanted any
thing from us now being an easy gale

July ye 3^{d} fryday This morning fine 8 a Clock weather saw a sail wch y^{e}
Bonadvent^{r}. bore away to & took her in a tow ye wind
springing up att East brough her away wth him &
kept all day ye hoy in a tow wth 2 hassers & a fine
fresh gale Easterly

July ye 4th Saturday This morning fair weath^{r}. ye wind took us short
about ten a Clock ye Com‸^{m}odore turn'd ye sweed away
who had given him an acco^{t}. y^{t} one of his men was ~~gone
along wth~~

[29]

gone along wth Mr Diberville & y^{t} he was gone wth 3
Saile

July ye 5th Sunday To day ye winds are ~~Vari~~‸^{a}~~ble~~ Continuing westerly sma[4]
breezes this four & twenty hours reeft topsailes a little
before night

July ye 6th Munday This day ye winds are Variable from ye S^{o}. West
to ye N^{o}. West fine Easy gales

July ye 7th Tuesday This day squally Weather till about 2 this after
noon ye wind dullered & veared about to ye N N E
a fine gale & our ship making more water then
Usual since this Last hard gale

July ye 8th Wednesday This morning Calm till eight & then small
Breezes from N^{o}. to ye W all day

July ye 9th Thursday This morning four o Clock fine Easy breeze
Notherly Continuing till towards ye Close of y^{e}
Evening growing calm we steered West a little North
erly all day

July ye 10th Friday To day steered west B N^{o}. small breezes from y^{e}
South to ye East towards Evening fell calm again

July ye 11^{h} Saturday This day small breezes Mixt wth Calmes about
ten this forenoon ye Commodores Boat came on board

1 Read by piecing together some loose scraps of paper.
2 Ibid.
3 Ibid.
4 Edge of paper frayed.

us inviting our Capt. thither to dinner wth ye Rest of ye Command^{rs}. Except Capt. Bayley being indisposed did not go ye rest tarrying there till Evening

July ye 12th Sunday Calm this morning ~~fair weather~~ & so Continuing westerly till about two this afternoon ye wind sprung up at N^{o} west at seven reeft topsails

July ye 13th Munday This morning fair Weather ye wind Continueing westerly tackt at four this morning this afternoon ye Deering brought to another Main top sail

July ye 14th Tuesday This morning fine weather till about noon it ~~blo~~ blowing fresh Reeft our topsales at two ye afternoon in ye Evening handed our maintopsail to day ~~brou~~ brought to a Mainsail Maintopsaile & Mizzen

[30]

July ye 15th Wednes This morning Tackt ye wind North^{r}ly & about eight this forenoon lay our Course W b N & a little afternoon Lett out our Reefes of topsails ye wind coming about N^{o}. Easterly wth fair weather

July ye 16th Thursd To day ye wind continuing ye same about N^{o}. E^{t}. fair weather we loosed our topgallentsailes & this Evening it proved very calm Latt^{de}. 58°" 1′7

July ye 17th friday This morning a fine Breeze at W S W & continued a fresh gale about ten reeft topsails now reckoning our selves about 50 Leagues of cape farewell veriation 18°" 0′0 this Evening ye Deering carry away his Mizzen yard

July ye 18th Saturday This morning it Blowed hard at W S W till about Evening it grew calm ye wind came up at N^{o} by E we steered away W N W Latt^{de}. 59°" 4′7

July ye 19th Sunday To day fine weather wth small Breezes at N^{o} N E till toward night it proved foggy about noon ye commodore seaford & deerings boats came on board ye seaford for some things they wanted

[31]

1694

A Journal of our wintering by gods assistance at hayes River in ye year of our Lord 1694

August ye 13th being Munday This day about noon ye ships weighed from ye rivers mouth it being ¾ flood & at high water ye wind being at S E ye albermarle broke her fast & drove upon ye ship but we gott her of again at 2 this afternoon our shallop came ashore ye ships being out of sight having two hands in ye marsh to look out

ye 14th Tuesday To day 3 of us was sent over ye River about 7 miles from ye house to keep an Eye abroad our people wen a rafting also

ye 22^{d} Wednesday This day ye gove^{r}nour sent a Boat to me wth 4^{lb} of powder & 20^{lb} of shott & 10 flints

ye 27th Munday This Evening ye Governour sent an Indian over to me wth ~~four~~ 4^{lb} of Powder & 20 lb of shott wth 10 flints

ye 28 Tuesday To day about noon I went home wth ye Indian y^{t} came last night & carryed wth us 19 geese

ye 29th Wednesday This morning I was sett over ye river in order to return to ye tent

Septr ye 1st Saturday This morning ye Blowed hard at N^{o}. W wth squals of snow being ye first we had this fall

ye 2^{d} Sunday To day another Boat from ye factory wth ~~four~~ 4^{lb} of Powder & 16 of shott wth 10 flints by wch I sent 17 Geese

ye 4th Tuesday This morning came a boat from ye house wth ye sam[1] quantity of powder & shott by which I sent 40 ge‸^{e}se

ye 5th Wednes I sent two hand wth our broken guns to be mended wch they did & returned in ye Evening

[32]

ye 11th Tuesday To day ye wind blowed very hard at N^{o}. W wth squals of snow

ye 12th Wednesday Last night it froze very hard & this morning much Ice lay along shore ye wind shifting from ye N^{o}. W to ye S^{o} W & fair weather

ye 13th Thursday To day ye Govern^{r}: sent two hands to relieve us in ye afternoon but we tarried this night

ye 14th friday This morning we set forth for ye house it blowing very hard northerly likewise snowing hard about noon gott to ye fort in ye Evening clearing up & indians being in ye marsh a hunting ‸^{brought}us news of two ships being arrived at Portnelson our people y^{t} were in ye marsh returning wth ye same news & one hand getting up ye flag stafe could disc‸^{r}y y^{m} from ye house this night watcht halfwatch

Septr ye 15th Saturday This morning ye Govern^{r}. sent two Indians over ye river wth a note for those two men wch was there Likewise another party of indians into ye marsh to make w^{t} discovery they could of ye french in ye afternoon they brought us

---

1 Edge of paper frayed.

news there was * 11 wch they saw but they told y^{m}
y^{t} there was forty of y^{m} landed so we broke
open small arms & gott our selves provided
for y^{m}

ye 16th Sunday To day about noon ye french came to ye woods
Edge & fired some guns at us & so went away we
have a discription y^{t} they have brought mohocks
we fired some guns into y^{e} woods

y^{e} 17th Munday This morning ten a Clock one of y^{e} ships
weighed from Portnelson & stood for our
River in y^{e} Evening came to anchor fair in
sight last night we fired sev$_{\wedge}^{er}$al guns to
scail y^{e} woods

[33]

~~York fort Hay~~

y^{e} 18th Tuesday Last night y^{e} wind blowing northerly it snowed
very hard about 11 a Clock we saw several men in y^{e}
woods Edge fireing at our people & they at y^{m} & one
great gun Likewise their boat came from
portnelson wth about 30 men great part of y^{m} landed
below ye fort & ye rest went aboard ye ship after w^{ch}
they went a sounding ye river this Evening ye ship
came into ye river & came to anchor 3 miles below y^{e}
house & landed some bundles on this side but could
not dicern w^{t} they were their people coming often
to larum us

ye 19th Wednesday This morning there Indians came within 2 miles
of ye fort there pitcht their tent at noon a Cannoe
arrived here Informing us y^{t} ye french had mortar
pieces on board & y^{t} they had seen y^{m} & y^{t} ye french Gover
ner told y^{m} y^{t} ye great should winter on ye north side
of portnelson they continue to alarum us this
Evening their ship weighed but soon after came aground
lying there y^{t} tide by reason their Boat was up ye river

ye 20th Thursday This morning their long boat went ashore some
Indians coming from ye other side ye river told us
she was loaden wth Boom shels & was going
to fetch ye morter Likewise some men went
along ye woods to guard y^{m} & in ye Evening ye boat
went ashore again loaden a wch we fired several
great guns they keeping a Party always to
alarum us

ye 21st Friday About noon their cannoes went a Boying &
sounding ye south Chanel at six this Evening almost
high water ye ship weighed & went up ye south chanel
at wch we fired 4 Great guns she got above ye fort
distance one mile & half & came aground much snow
last night & Ice drove in ye river

[34]

Septr. ye 22^{d} Saturday To day ye ship continued aground ye Ice growing thicker they lightened their ship wth ye long boat they

~~*ye 23^{d} Sunday*~~

ye 23^{d} Sunday Keeping hands alwayes to alarum us
This morning they gott of their ship & stood for ye north shoar but being hindered by ye Ice came aground again but seeing our people fetching of wood came & shott at y^{m} but did no hurt

ye 24th Munday Last night gott their ship of & warpt ashore about a mile & half above ye fort to day at low water we see y^{m} hand deal Boards & other goods ashore their people still alarum us

ye 25th Tuesday To day we could discry nothing but their securing their ship

ye 26th Wednesd To day at noon our ~~people said~~ ^Yacht drove^ away to ye other side of ye river much Ice being in ye other chanel drove to sea out of sight

ye 27th thursday Last night our people said they saw some french men so fired some guns this morning saw one more plain fired one gun at him

ye 28th friday This day we saw ye french gett their goods ashore

ye 29th Saturday This morning they came so near us y^{t} we saw y^{m} fall trees & at noon came to ye woods edge & fired at our people all ye afternoon we firing now & then again when we could see y^{m}

ye 30th Sunday Last night our people saw a man & fired at him this afternoon happened an Imbroile in ye fort Joseph stays more being ye cause thereof ye french came to ye woods Edge our people shott at y^{m}

[35]

October ye 1st Munday About ten oClock this morning came an Indian who told us y^{t} he came from above ye french but meeting wth one of y^{m} in ye woods carryed him to ye ship he said y^{t} morning they gott ashore their Boom & was Intended to play it shortly & this Evening fired their Boom but it fell three or four hundrd yards short we seeing y^{m} in ye woods edge fired 2 muskets at y^{m} so gave ye Indian some Oatmel & sent him away

ye 2^{d} Tuesday Last night they made great fires near us about five hundred yards to day came to ye woods Edge & fired 3 guns at us & this Evening they put up flag staves at ye mast head of ye ship & kept their fire day & night

Octr ye 3^{d} Wednesday To day about noon came one french man & a ~~mohaw~~ mohawk Indian wth a flag of truce wth a summons to our governour wch spacefied y^{t} they was ready to

Cannonade & Boombard ye fort & if we would
not surrender it they would reduce it to ashes &
give us no quarter so desired our answer by
Eight a Clock ye next morning so ye Govern^{r}.
desired longer time to Consider of it but they
would not so he sent y^{m} word he would

ye 4th Thursday

This morning M^{r}. Matthew & I went wth a flag
of truce & carryed our articles wch their cheif
perrused then those wch he did not like altered so
demanded ye governour to surrender it up at
4 a Clock in ye afternoon forasmuch a he would
not alter[1] his Resolution but would begin to
play when ye time was Expired Likewise he allotted
us ye house called foxhall to put all our things
in so we returned at ten & gott our things in
order & at 12 he sent two men to hear our ans
wer so ye Govern^{r}. told y^{m} since he could have no

[36]

longer time would make ready for his Entrance
so accordingly they came & took possession of y^{e}
fort our Govern^{r}. & 14 more of us was ordered to go
up to M^{r}. Diberveall house in order to pass y^{e}
night

To Clark	1
To bennet	1
To Witham	1
To Young	1
To Pratt	1
To Moor	1
To Dix	1
To Paul	1
To Pitts	1

	£
To Candles	22
To Cheese	28
To soap	120
To Sugar	28

To Brandy 6 gallons
To Cardymum & Carnaway waters 4 Gallons
To 2 Ounces of sowing silk 2 ounces stiching
sweet herbs & spices black silk & ^{124} buttons 144

1 The "l" resembles an "f".

[37]

1696

A Journal of wintering by gods assistance
at Hayes river in ye year one Thousand
six hundred Ninety Six Septr ye 18th

friday Sept^{r}ye 18th this morning dispatcht ye Hudsonsbay & about 10 this forenoon she sailed from before ye factory & went down to lower five fathom hole ye govern^{r}. sent a boat aboard wch returned about nine this Even^{g}: told us y^{t} at low water she grounded & sued about 2 foot ye wind being N^{o}.therly & thick weather could not see where to come to anchor we have had no news from ye ships lowest down since they went out this night watcht quarter watch ye 16th Instant Bowatter lost his thumb

Satturday Septr. ye 19th to day about ten this forenoon ye Hudsonsbay weighed & went out to ye other ships Likewise cap^{t}. Grimmington came up wth a boat to sattisfie ye Govern^{r}. w^{t} he had put aboard ye knig^{ht} to go down into ye Bay & Likewise told ye Govern^{r}. y^{t} reason of his going out without orders was y^{t} ye Commodore Command^{d}. him to goe out & y^{t} his orders was to take him along wth him therefore bid him not stay behind at his perril so ye Govr. desired him to sail as soon as possible he went from us about noon we have had Indians here this two days past sent one cannoe up ye river to see if deer ~~had~~ crost & ye rest to portnelson to see w^{t} news there our ships remained at anchor all day ye wind S^{o}.therly

~~Tuesday~~ ^Sunday ye 20th this morning all ye ships sailed Except ye knight & she sailed about ten this forenoon

[38]

ye wind being W^{t}.erly a fresh gale this afternoon ye Cannoe I sent up ye river came back & said ye deer had done passing this river some time since to day was found some catridges of Powder but it was wet

Munday ye 21st this morn^{g}. ye Govr. send 2 hands over ye river to ye albemarle to unbend her sails & to see w^{t} Condition she is in about noon came some Indians out of portnelson wth whom I traded some beavour today we got all ye old cask & placed round ye foundation of ye lower platform & filled y^{m} wth stones & this Even^{g}. ye Indians went all away Except Guyers Child wch we kept ye wind N^{o}therly & freezing hard

Tuesday ye 22^{d} fair weath^{r}. frosty this morn^{g}. Mr Kelsey wth 2 hands went up ye river in a Cannoe to try to take some fish sent some hands up also to make a Raft of of firewood who return'd being near in ye Evening our people shot 2 Geese near ye plantation ye wind continues in ye N W Quadr'^{t}.

Wednesday 23 wind & Weath^{r}. continuing some of our men went up to work on ye raft firewood ye gov^{r}. sent away two hands to Portnelson river we are now fixing up at home our Lodging

Thursday 24th Moderate frost little wind to day about nine forenoon came to ye fort having had no success Mr Newton & another hand being gone over ye river to a smoke wch was seen all night when returning again brought news y^{t} ye seafords pinnace wth nine men was drove from ye ships ye 19th day at night & gott ashore on ye south

[39]

shore five of y^{m} being come wth our people y^{t} went to ye albamarle Mr Newton brought our two men over ~~at~~ in ~~flood~~ ye Cannoe so sent ye pinnace over at flood for those men likewise sent our two men away wth provision to see for ye other four this afternoon came one Indian from portnelson who said there was more a coming this evening he went back to his cannoe to day we begun to set up palesadoes round ye gov^{rs}. house took acco^{t} of ye trading room

friday ye 25th ye weath^{r}. continuing this morn^{g}. sent five hands into ye marsh to ye Indian y^{t} was here last night to help bring his deers flesh & at ye same time came two indians out of ye woods loaden wth meat & at 11 a Clock traded their meat & Beavour this afternoon our pinnace went down where ye ships rid & brought wth y^{m} a hasser & anchor & said there was ye Commodores small bower & a hasser remaining our people at work still to set up palesadoes

Saturday ye 26th this morn^{g}. hard frost ice drove in ye river ye indians y^{t} came yesterday went away about ten this forenoon our pinnace went down again & brought wth y^{m} an anchor & piece of hasser wch we Judged to be ye deerings likewise our shallop went a creeping for an anchor against ye fort hooked but hauling it up brake ye creeper to day buried 6 ~~Barrels~~ Barrels of Beer our people continues about ye palasadeos this afternoon ye wind came about Easterly a moderate Gale no news from ye other side

Sunday ye 27th Cloudy weath^{r}. wth small ~~breezes~~ ^snow ye wind N^{o}therly this afternoon was found 9

[40]

Catridges of powder & one sack of wheat no news from y^{e} other side

Munday y^{e} 28th it snowed hard last night so this Morn^{g}. our hands went to setting up y^{e} wood into a pile about noon our pinnace went down to where we played y^{e} mortar & fetcht one ~~mortor~~$_{\wedge}$^{anchor}& hasser wch y^{e} seaford left y^{e} anchor y^{e} Hudsons bay

Tuesday y^{e} 29th this morning y^{e} Ice was very thick in y^{e} River got up y^{e} rest of our wood & likewise haul'd up our Boats & got all y^{e} anchors up to high water mark this afternoon our 2 men returned from y^{e} other side wth y^{e} yaul bringing news y^{t} they found no men but Judged y^{m} to be dead by reason they found a bone & sleave of a shirt all bloody y^{e} bone they b$_{\wedge}$^{r}ought wth y^{m} our Churgeon said he thought it to be y^{e} bone of a mans arm moderate weath^{r}. y^{e} wind S^{o}therly gave our men out Indian shoes

Wednesday y^{e} 30th Last night it snowed hard y^{e} wind E^{t}erly this morn^{g}. sent our people to cut wood & pile it up near y^{e} bank side in case we should want in ye winter about nine this forenoon they came home it continuing snow ing hard went no more but went to pointing our Houses & altering their lodgings

[41]

Thursday Octob^{r}. y^{e} 1st y^{e} weath^{r}. continues wth y^{e} wind between y^{e} N^{o}. & y^{e} East a hard gale to day gott up our other boat & y^{e} men kept pointing y^{e} houses

Fri$_{ri}$day y^{e} 2^{d} to day made an end of pointing y^{e} houses y^{e} weather continuing blowing & snowing the wind coming to y^{e} westward of y^{e} north

saturday y^{e} 3^{d} moderate weather little wind our people took up stockings and shoe clouts

Sunday y^{e} 4th fair weather the wind between the south & ye East a strong gale froze very hard last night

Munday ye 5th fair weather some of our people went out ahunting & saw some Deers tracks & found ye legs of one which the wolves had kill'd but discover'd nothing at port nelson

Tuesday ye 6th fresh gales of wind from ye west N^{o}W^{t} to ye N^{o}.W^{t} this morning I & 3 of our men went 9 miles up ye river to see for fish ye rest of our hands went to cut wood near ye house

Wednesday ye 7th to day strong gales of wind at

N^{o}.W^{t}. wth small snow our people continue to cut wood

Thursday ye 8th wind & weather continue & our men wooding as formerly

friday ye 9th fine weather ye wind Ditto this day ye south Channel stopt wth Ice & ye River froze over at Gooseberrys house where I was so I sent 2 men down to ye fort wth 2

[42]

Saturday ye 10th Moderate Weath^{r}. ye winds D^{o}. to day ye 2 men returned to me & brought wth y^{m} one more

Sunday ye 11th fair weather ye wind between the south & the west some small snow fell this morn^{g}.

Munday the 12th the wind variable from the S^{o}. W^{t}. to ye S^{o}.E^{t}. snowing weather 10 of our men went ~~out~~‸ over ~~ahunting~~‸ the river to ye fourteens to hunt & fish & 3 of our men went out ahunting returned in ye Even^{g}. bringing 7 patridges

Tuesday ye 13th this morning snowed ye wind Wst.erly 3 of our people went out a hunting brought home one patridge we Likewise discovered some deer tracks & our people shott at some one martin catcht to day being ye first

Wednesday ye 14th fresh gales of wind from ye N^{o}. to ye Wst. to day 5 of our men went a hunting but caught nothing Likewise we all went a hunting & I kill'd 2 deer

Thursday ye 15th Cloudy weath^{r}. ye wind between ye S^{o}. & ye E^{t} wth snow to day some of our people going a hunting came up wth some deer & shott at y^{m} but did not kill Likewise we went out & one of y^{m} kill'd a deer 2 of our men was lost from ye factory

friday ye 16th weather Ditto some of our men went a hunting & withall to look for the men wch was lost

Saturday ye 17th Clear weather ye wind from ye S^{o}. to ye Wst. some of our men went a hunting & brought home 4 patridges & some came home from ye fourteens & brought 20 trouts I sent 3 men home wth 2 Deers heads & some deers flesh

[43]

Sunday ye 18th moderate weath^{r}. ye wind ditto to day ye men returned wth more men to fetch ye remaining part of ye deer & 2 Indians came to y^{e} factory from up portnelson River

Munday y^{e} 19th to day I sent y^{e} men home wth y^{e} deer some of our men went a hunting one of y^{e} Indians returned having traded y^{e} other y^{e} other remained at y^{e} factory y^{e} former lay at my tent wth me

Tuesday y^{e} 20th y^{e} wind S^{o}.the$_{\wedge}^{r}$ly some of our men & y^{e} Indian went a hunting but returned having seen no game but one man lost himself

Wednesday y^{e} 21st y^{e} winds & weath^{r}. variable from y^{e} N^{o}. W^{t}. to y^{e} N^{o}. E^{t}. some snow to day some of our people & y^{e} Indian went out to look for y^{e} lost he & they returned wth 5 patridges to day I removed our selves to ten shilling ~~river~~ Creek

Thursday ye 22^{d} ye weather ditto ye wind from ye S^{o} W^{t} to ye N^{o}. E^{t}. N^{o}.therly to day some men & Y^{e} Indian went a hunting returned wthout game only ye Indian Kill'd one Rabbit & a patridge to day set 21 hooks for fish

friday ye 23^{d} fair weather nothing remarkable

Saturday ye 24th this morning took up all ye hooks & went all home to the factory snowing squally weath^{r}. ye wind S^{o}.therly ye Indian being out return'd in ye afternoon wth 3 patridges

[44]

Sunday ye 25th strong gales of wind at N^{o}. with snow sent ye Indian over to our people at ye fourteens to hear w^{t} news & in ye Even^{g}. ye gunner another hand & ye Indian returned they brought with them 10 trout

Munday ye 26th Clear weather ye wind ditto 3 of our men came from ye fourteens for provision and brought ~~with them~~ one fish to day the S^{o}. Channel fastened again with Ice

Tuesday the 27th moderate gales the weather Ditto this day I and those men which came from the fourteens and 3 more men which stayed at the french Creek to fish the rest returned to the fourteens four more going Likewise up the River to hunt and fish

Wednesday the 28th fine weather the wind S^{o}. E^{t}. to day one of our men went a hunt ing but caught nothing

Thursday the 29th Variable winds from the S^{o} E^{t}. to the N^{o}. W^{t}.with much snow to day shot 5 wood patridges in the plan

friday the 30th strong gales of wind with small snow one of our men went a hunting no success

[45]

Saturday y^{e} 31st fair weather the wind S^{o} W^{t}. I and some of the men from the fourteens came home bringing 10 fish and 19 patridges and one hand from the house 2 more ditto

Likewise 2 hands $_{\wedge}^{\text{came}}$ from above having nothing
this week

Sunday november y^{e} 1st moderate weather
the wind S^{o} W^{t}. this day came 3 men from
the french Creek and in y^{e} afternoon came
two hands from y^{e} fourteens bringing
with them two mohawks who said they left
some Indians six days since that wanted
victuals and were coming towards the
fort

Munday the 2^{d} fair weather the wind
S^{o}therly to day some of our men and one
of the Mohawks with the Indian went
returned to the fourteens one of our men
went a hunting and Killed six
patridges

Tuesday the 3^{d} strong gales of wind S^{o}therly
Clear weather to day the rest of our men
returned to the fourteens and one came
from thence another went up the River to
see for the 2 men y^{t} is there some of our men
went a hunting but caught nothing

[46]

Wednesday the 4th fair weather the winds
variable from the S^{o} W^{t} to the N^{o} E^{t} to day
our men that was up the river came home
having caught nothing and one hand
went to the fourteens and some went a
hunting brought home about 10 patrid^{ges}

Thursday the 5th strong gales of wind
from the S^{o}. to the E^{t} Cloudy weath^{r}.

friday the 6th Clear weather the wind
ditto two of our men went a hunting towards
the fourteens and some on this side
which brought about 12 patridges

Saturday the 7th some snow last night
the wind N^{o}.therly some of our men
came from the fourteens and brought
with them 98 patridges some men went
a hunting brought one ditto and one new
gun broak

Sunday the 8th fair weather 2 of the
Indians went a hunting and brought
14 patridges this morning 8 a Clock
Matthew Vickary died

Munday the 9th thick weather this
morning at noon Cleared up two
hands came from ye french Creek
the Indians went a hunting brought

[47]

home 2 patridges and one Rabbit this
afternoon buried our man

Tuesday the 10th Moderate gales between
the N^{o}. and the W^{t} with small snow to
day the two men returned to the french
Creek and I with one of our men and
2 Indians went a Beavour hunting
2 of our men went from the fort
a hunting but caught nothing

Wednesday the 11th Wind and weather
Ditto our men went to fetch home
wood and one hand went a
hunting brought home 2 patridges

Thursday the 12th clear weather
wind ditto our people Continue to
fetch wood and one of our men went
a hunting kill'd 2 patridges

Friday the 13th wind ditto some
snow nothing remarkable but one of
our men went ~~a hunting~~ out and
kil'd 5 patridges

[48]

Saturday the 14th moderate gales west
erly some snow to day 5 of ~~of~~ our men
came from the fourteens which brought
7 Jacks and 20 patridges likewise
two from the french Creek with 2
Jack and two trout

Sunday the 15th fine clear weath^{r}.
with little wind ditto our men returned
from beavour hunting having caught
one and 8 patridges this morning between
12 & 1 Daniel Hardy died

Munday the 16th fair weather to
day our men returned to the fourteens
and likewise to the french creek this
afternoon buried our man

Tuesday the 17th Moderate
weather the wind N^{o}.therly this
morning came 2 Indians starved
to the fort having left their family's
2 days Journey of Likewise 2 of
our men went to the fourteens one
of which returned again in the
Evening and one hand went a hunting
brought home 6 patridges

[49]

Wednesday the 18th last night some

snow the wind N^{o}therly to day the Indian returned to his family with some Indian corn the other and one of our men went a hunting brought home 13 patridges likewise one Indian came from our people at the fourteens

Thursday the 19th Last night Edward Harrington dyed to day we Buried him 2 Indians went a hunting brought 22 patridges moderate weath er little wind

Friday the 20th Last night 11 a Clock came 2 Indians to the fort from the other side the river one being the same that went away to meet the family and to day the rest came to ye factory 2 Indians and one of our men went a hunting brought home 24 patridges this Evening some snow wind N^{o}therly

Saturday the 21st Last night the River fastened against the fort to day some of our people came from the fourteens and Likewise some from the french

[50]

Creek brought with them 6 patridges and four fish some of our men went a hunting brought 20 patridges clear weather little wind between the N^{o}. & ye west

Sunday the 22^{d} some snow the Wind N^{o}therly to day came 3 Indians from between portnelson and this River 2 days Journey brought some Beaver

Munday the 23^{d} moderate gales at W N W weather ditto to day our men returned to the fourteens and french Creek and 3 or 4 of our men went with them to fall timber and to hunt beavour 2 Indians and one of our men went a hunting brought 15 patridges

Tuesday the 24th this day wind S^{o} W^{t}. the Indians went from the fort and carryed with them those that came here starved to day two of our men went to the fourteens

one of which tarryed there Likewise
3 indians came to the fort one of
which was the french Captain they
brought nothing but 2 white fox skins

[51]

Wednesday the 25th strong gales at
N N W^{t} to day the french Captain
and the Indians went from the fort
2 of our men went a hunting brought
15 patridges

Thursday the 26^{t} moderate gales
W N W^{t} to day our men fetcht home
wood from the Creek above the
house and the indian went a
hunting kill'd 5 patridges

Friday the 27th cloudy weath^{r}.
the wind W^{t} to day I came home
with an Indian having set our
people about the timber but
caught no beaver

Saturday the 28th Clear weath^{r}.
the wind S^{o}therly to day some
of our people came from the
fourteens ~~for our~~ and the french
creek brought 2 patridges

Sunday ye 29th some snow last night
the wind came about N^{o}.therly to day
sent one Indian to ye fourteens for our
beaver nets & ice Chizzels

[52]

Munday the 30th Moderate weath
er our people returned to the four
teens and the french Creek our
men went a hunting brought 7
patridges

Tuesday ~~the~~ December the 1st
this morning I and Mr Newton
went toward portnelson to see
what we could discover but it
came on snowy and thick weather
so we returned gott home at
night the wind between the S^{o}.
and the East our people kill'd
7 patridges

Wednesday the 2^{d} some small
snow the wind between the
S^{o} and the W^{t}. this morning 2
hands went to the fourteens
our people went a hunting kill'd
16 patridges

Thursday the 3^{d} Cloudy
weather wind W^{t}. this Morning
2 hands ~~went~~ came from the four
teens saying they began sawing

[53]

yesterday Likewise our people went
a hunting and killed ^about 16 patridges

Friday the 4th the wind between
the S^{o}. and the E^{t}. weather Ditto our
people went a hunting brought
8 patridges and one Rabbit this
Evening the same Indian that
was here starved that went away
came again having left his family
this morning and some other
Indians a thursday

Saturday the 5th strong gales of
wind N^{o}.therly to day some of
our people came from the fourteens
and french Creek

Sunday the 6 Clear weather
the wind variable from the
N^{o}. to the S^{o} W^{t}

Munday the 7th weather ditto
the wind West to day our
people returned to the fourteens
and french creek Likewise here

[54]

came 3 Indians starved to the fort
our people went a hunting brought
29 patridges saw a smoke on the
south side sent a hand to know
the reason proved to be the
mohawks

Tuesday the 8th wind and weath^{r}.
the same our hunters kill'd 7
patridges and one white fox the
rest of our people fetcht home wood

Wednesday the 9th Clear weath^{r}.
the wind between the N^{o}. and
the W^{t}. to day those Indians that
came last went away and the
other Indians that came a friday
last his family gott hither our
people continue to fetch wood

Thursday the 10th fresh gales
N^{o}.therly thick weather our
people still fetch wood our
hunters kill'd to day 13
patridges

Friday the 11th fresh gales at
N W wth drift

[55]

Saturday the 12th Clear weather the
wind west our people some from the
french creek and the fourteens
brought 41 patridges our hunters
Likewise killed 38

Sunday the 13th fair weather
the wind ditto to day saw one man
cross the river above the fort 2
mile sent two indians to discover the
track returning told us it was a
man without snow shoes here came
also an indian woman with 2
children for relief having left 5 more
Indians that was coming also the
12 Instant

Munday the 14th fair weather
little wind to day our people
returned to the fourteens and
french Creek our hunters kill'd
29 patridges

Tuesday the 15th Moderate
weather the wind Easterly
I and one Mohawk went over
the River to set a nett the same
day came 8 Indians to the
fort 3 of which had been here
before

[56]

Wednesday the 16th Cloudy weather
the wind North West returned to
the house having catcht one Jack
to day our hunters kill'd 30
patridges and 3 Rabbits

Thursday the 17th fair weath^{r}.
little wind our hunters kill'd ~~30~~
17 patridges & one rabbit

Friday the 18th thick weath^{r}.
the wind S^{o}.therly our hunters
kill'd 30 patridges and found
one wolf

Saturday the 19th wind and
Weather ditto to day our people
came all home from the
fourteens and french Creek
Likewise 6 indians went away
our people brought 93 patridges

our hunters kill'd 34 and 3
rabbits

Sunday the 20th some snow
the wind N^{o}. this morning
came 3 indians starved
likewise sent two up the
river to fish & hunt

[57]

Munday the 21st Wind and weath^{r}.
Ditto our hunters kill'd 21 patridges
& one Rabbit

Tuesday the 22^{d} strong gales
of wind N^{o}.therly and much
Drift

Wednesday the 23^{d} Clear weath^{r}.
the wind W^{t}. our hunters kill'd
25 patridges

Thursday the 24th fair weath^{r}.
the wind Wst. to day our hunters
kill'd 9 patridges one Indian
dyed fetcht wood home

Friday the 25th Wind &
weather Ditto last night they
burnt the Corps to day came y^{e}
black boy and his wife to the fort
Likewise whiskers came from his
family an returned in the even
ing black boy brought our gun
splitt

Saturday the 26th fine weather
the wind W^{t}erly this morning
came all whiskers family to
the fort

Sunday the 27th fresh gales at S^{o}
W^{t}. wth drift

[58]

Munday the 28th fine gales ditto
Clear to day made a search found
some trading goods in the mens
chest of which the governer took $_{\wedge}$^{an} acco^{t}.
this Evening some difference fell
between the governer and Mr Newton
upon which the Governer turned
him out of place and his house

Arrabeck or indian language of hudsons
bay$_{bay}$

[1]Cakiththa keeshquebbaujwahtchee j aihttee naunneewee Ne wee No tee Squea wan Kescot nee Kiththee Chua quoaming Pee lanee ma Newa Wha pimmok Kagi a Nee pa autta Meshshee woan poos co Tabbiscanura[d]

Tuesday the 29th small snow the wind N°therly our indians and one English man went a hunting kill'd 10 patridges and 4 rabbits to day the governer took from Andrew Johnson all his beaver by reason he traded some of it with an indian called whiskers Likewise some small matter of Beaver stones that is about 6 Beaver and as many stones one indian & one English man went to ye fourteens

[59]

Wednesday the 30th Clear weather the wind ditto our indians went a hunting and kill'd 11 patridges

Thursday the 31st strong gales of wind N°.therly with drift to day our man and the indian returned from the fourteens but had no success

A pleasant fancy of old time which made me write in an unknown tongue because counsel is kept best in one single Breast[2] vale

1697

1697[6] Friday January the 1st. clear weather the wind Wterly this morning 2 mohawks and one other indian set out for the ~~nort~~ North side of portnelson to hunt patridges and 2 more Ditto to hunting about the fort the latter brought 3 patridges to day was found 3 cask of beaver shott knives and flints awls and steels that the french had hid under the floor of one of the cabbins and over the Ceiling

---

1 The Indian words which follow are written with a finer pen, but perhaps by the same hand, as the remainder of the text. The transcription here given is in many places uncertain.

2 In the original this passage is opposite the Indian words on page 58.

[60]

Saturday the 2^{d} Gloomy weather
the westerly one English man and
1 Indian went a hunting had no
success to day our people fetcht home
all the fire wood we had cut in y^{e}
woods

Sunday the 3^{d} fair $weath^{r}$.
the wind W^{t}. this morning
black boy and his wife went
to lye out two or 3 nights one
Indian went a hunting had
no game

Munday the 4th wind &
weather ditto to day 8 of our
m~~a~~$_{\wedge}^{e}$n went to the fourteens
to saw and hunt sent over
another saw to keep two saws
going

Tuesday the 5th Clear
Weather wind between the
S^{o} and the W^{t}. this morning
our men went about cleaning
the yard afternoon our 3
Indians returned from the N^{o}
side of portnelson brought
about 15 patridges one indian
went a hunting near home but had
no success

[61]

Wednesday the 6th Clear weather
wind S^{o}.therly we made an End
of cleaning the yard 2 English
men went a hunting kill'd one
patridge

Thursday the 7th thick $weath^{r}$.
wind Easterly this morning
went to the fourteens took 2 hands
along with mee to try to draw
home plank but could not so came
with one upon the dogs slead to the
Rivers side the wind being about
N^{o}.therly advised them to
return to the fourteens told
them they would not hold it over
it drift so hard they said they could
gott in sight of the north shore
one began to faint I ordered the
other to stay with him till I
went to the house and sent relief
but before our people gott to them

it being almost dark Rich^{d}. bean
was almost dead and Wm Howard
destracted so was forc'd to sent many
men to fetch them both home
having left the plant about ¾ of a
Mile of Rich^{d}. beans hands was

[62]

froze much his face Likewise could
not speak when brought home the
others face a little 1 English man
and 2 Indians went a hunting
Kill 17 patridges

Friday the 8th fair weather
the wind between the N^{o}. and
the W^{t}. to day 4 Indians and
one English man went a hunting
kill'd 15 patridges and 2 rabits

Saturday the 9th thick weath^{r}.
the wind N^{o}.therly small
snow to day 3 hands came
from the fourteens one English
man and five Indians went
a hunting kill'd 29 patridges
& 1 Rabbit

Sunday the 10th fair weath^{r}.
wind W^{t}.

Munday the 11th Clear
weather the wind W^{t}. 4
Indians & one English man went
a hunting kill'd 7 patridges to day
our people returned to ye fourteens

[63]

Tuesday the 12^{t} Wind and weath^{r}.
Ditto 2 Indians went a hunting
kill'd 5 patridges

Wednesday the 13th small snow
the wind between the N^{o}. and the
E^{t}. with drift one English man
and 5 Indians went a hunting
Killd 9 rabbits and 3 patridges
one of the Indians went to lye
out a night or two to make snow shoes

Thursday the 14th fresh gales
at ~~N~~^{o}. W^{t} ·Clear weathr.

Friday the 15th fresh gales
at N^{o}. W^{t}. 2 English men
and 4 indians Likewise the
other returned from Lying
out brought home in all 35
patridges & one Rabbitt

Saturday the 16th Clear
weather the wind Ditto to day
came 5 hands from the fourteens
4 Indians went a hunting kill'd
9 patridges this morning 2 a Clock
Died Rich^{d}. Beaver our Chirur
geon opened his breast found
Several of his Ribs broak wch Edwd. Harrington
did while Living

[64]

Sunday the 17th snowy weath^{r}.
the wind between the S^{o}. and
the W^{t}. till Evening wind N^{o}.
blew hard

Munday the 18th much wind
N^{o}.therly and drift insomuch
that our people could not return
to ye fourteens

Tuesday the 19th thick
weather the wind from
the S^{o}. E^{t}. to the W^{t}. this morning
our people returned to the
fourteens at noon fitted 17
indians with 10 days provisions
and sent them away to look
for deer this afternoon buried
Rich^{d}. Beaver one English man
and one Indian went to lye
out at ten shilling Creek a night
or two to kill patridges two
indians went likewise to the
fourteens to do the same and
one Indian went from the
house Kill'd 6 patridges

Wednesday the 20th a storm of
wind N^{o}.therly with much
drift

[65]

Thursday the 21st fresh gale
of wind Ditto and drift our
English man and Indian return'd
this afternoon had no success

Friday the 22^{d} fair weather
the wind W^{t}. 2 Indians went
a hunting 2 of the 17 Indians
returned one English man went
to see if ye Rest were gone another
went with a note to the fourteens
returned in the Evening

Saturday the 23^{d} Cloudy weath

er wind Est.erly 5 hands came
from the fourteens brought 22
patridges 2 Indians went a
hunting kill'd 1 patridge

Sunday the 24th thick ~~weath~~
weather wind S^{o}.therly our 2
Indians came from the four
teens brought 14 patridges

Munday the 25th Clear
weather the wind ditto to
day our people and the 2 indians
returned to ye fourteens 2 indians
went a hunting from ye fort
kill'd 4 patridges

[66]

Tuesday the 26 Hazy warm
weather the wind strong S^{o}therly
the 2 Indians that came back
the other day set out this morn^{g}
to follow the Rest one of our
Indians went to lye out and
one English man went a hunt
ing kill'd 2 patridges

Wednesday the 27th wind
from the S^{o}. to the W^{t}. weath^{r}.
ditto to day came one Indian
came from the fourteens brought
20 patridges one English and
2 Indians went a hunting
kill'd 5 patridges the Indian
getting what he came for
return'd to the fourteens our
people heaving the snow
of all the flankers

Thursday the 28th last
night strong gales N^{o}.therly
with snow and so remained
all day

[67]

Friday the 29th Moderate
weather wind Easterly with
small snow our people went to
cleaning the yard but left when
snowed 2 indians went to hunt
kill'd 4 patridges

Saturday the 30th Clear
weather wind S^{o} E^{t}. 3 English
and 2 Indians came from the
fourteens brought with them
47 patridges and 4 Rabbits

one English and 2 Indians
to hunt from the fort kill'd
17 patridges & Rabbits 2 our
men cleaned the yard

Sunday the 31st strong
gales at N°.Et. and East
with snow

Munday ~~the~~ February
the 1st wind Ditto much
drift our people returned to
the fourteens & 3 Indians went
there also to hunt a deer wch was seen
Saturday last

[68]

Tuesday the 2d wind and
weather Ditto one English went
a hunting had no success

Wednesday the 3d fresh gales
Ditto Clear sent one hand
to the fourteens to hear what news
and one Indian killd 2 patridges

Thursday the 4th wind
West our man returned from
the fourteens and one Indian
which brought 2 patridges
and one Rabbit one Indian a
hunting kill'd 2 Rabbit &
one patridge

Friday the 5th Clear
wind S° Wt. 2 Indians went a
hunting kill'd 8 patridges Thos. Dutton
went out Likewise splitt his piece &
hurt his hand & froze it also

Saturday the 6t wind &
weather ditto our men came all
home from the fourteens one indian
came round a hunting kill'd 7
patridges 2 indians out a hunting
had no success

[69]

Sunday the 7th weather Ditto little wind
Wt.erly

Munday the 8th weather Ditto wind N°.
Wt. I and 2 Indians went to lie out
one the North side of portnelson to
kill patridges ye 2 Mohawks likewise
on ye same accot. to ten shilling Creek

Tuesday the 9th wind N°.Wt. snow
& drift

Wednesday the 10th moderate gales W^{t}.N^{o}.W^{t}. wth small snow till noon then Clear

Thursday ye 11th wind & weather ditto Clear this morn^{g}. whiskers came to the factory starved gives a very lamentable relation of those indians y^{t} went hence wth him Likewise an upland Indian & his wife came to ye fort from up this river wch traded some beaver our mohawks returned wth 23 patridges our men cleaned ye yard

friday ye 12^{t} little wind S^{o}.W^{t}. & smal snow our men continue at ye same about ye pallasadoes our hunters kill'd 10 patridges & 1 Rabbit & we returned in Evening brought 69 patridges ye uplander & his wife went away

[70]

Saturday the 13th fair weath^{r}. wind N^{o}.W^{t}.

Sunday ye 14th wind N^{o}.E^{t}. snow & drift whiskers returned to his family wth oatmeal & pease not to bring y^{m} to ye fort

Munday ye 15th weath^{r}. Clear wind N^{o}.therly 2 English & 4 Indians went to ye N^{o}. side of portnelson ye rest of our men went to cut wood & fetcht it home for the fire from the back of the house

Tuesday ye 16th Little wind weath^{r} ditto one hand went to ye french creek returned at Even^{g}. ye Govr. & Mr Newton having words turn'd him out of ‸^{his} house & took ~~from him~~ the keys of ye Warehouse from him having not been himself since sunday night & not without Just cause

[71]

Wednesday ye 17th thick wind between ye S^{o} & ye E^{t}. our men fetching fire wood home this Even^{g}. came one Indian to ye fort being ye french cap^{ts}. son little nest who said his wife was coming wth whiskers family hither

Thursday y^{e} 18th Clear weath^{r}. ~~ditto~~ ‸^{wind} ~~our~~ W^{t}.erly friday y^{e} 19th wind & weath^{r}. ditto our fetcht home wood & those wch went to y^{e} other side of portnelson return'd brought 86 patridges this Even^{g}. whiskers $_{\wedge}$$^{\&\ his}$ family came to y^{e} fort y^{e} Govr. beat him & turn'd him out for abusing us in giving a token sent to me he giving it to one of our men & likewise has been a plague to us all this winter in being lazy 2 English men out to day caught nothing

Saturday the 20th wind & weather Ditto 2 indians a hunting kill'd 9 patridges

Sunday ye 21st wind N^{o}W^{t}. & Clear

[72]

Munday the 22^{d} fair weath^{r}. wind ditto 4 hands went to ye N^{o}. side of portnelson & 4 more to ye fourteens to fish & hunt ye rest went to fetch wood

Tuesday the 23^{d} to day I & another English wth four indians set out for ye N^{o}. side of portnelson to hunt deer

Wednesday the 24th wind & weath^{r}. ditto

Thursday ye 25th little wind fine weather our men went to wood & ye french Cap^{ts}. son & his wife went from the factory this Even^{g}.

friday the 26 moderate weath^{r}. wind ditto our men went a ~~hunting~~ wooding

Saturday ye 27th wind S^{o}W^{t}. this Day & yesterday the snow gave about the house our men went a wooding & those men returned from the french Creek but caught no fish & our hunters from portnelson brought 80 patridges

[73]

Sunday ye 28th moderate gales W^{t}. N^{o}.W^{t}. the snow melted about ye factory &c

Munday the ~~29th~~ 1st of March
little wind S^{o}therly it continues
thawing this Evening 2 indians
came to ye factory and the french
cap^{ts}. son that went away thursday
night returned with them they
all say it has been a very hard
winter however they presented
the Govr. with some tongues
& heads &c

Tuesday the 2^{d} snow & drift
wind N^{o}.W^{t}. the 3 Indians went
from the factory but the french
cap^{ts}. sons wife stayed here being
lame

Wednesday the 3^{d} moderate gales
ditto ^{to}day our ^^{men} went to woods this
Evening the dog slouch came up
with 2 wolves on the river fought
them both half an hour but
our men not coming to his
assistance they left him he not
being able to fight them any^ ^{longer}

[74]

to day 2 men returned from the
deer hunters ^$^{~~longer~~ being}$ not able to perform

Thursday the 4th wind S^{o}therly
thawy to day our men heaved y^{e}
snow out of y^{e} palasadoes

Friday the 5th wind N^{o}.W^{t}.
blowed hard last night and
to day Drift & snowed exceedingly
this day 3 indians came to y^{e}
factory and traded some skins
and went away in the Even^{g}.

Saturday the 6th wind N^{o}.therly
hard gales with snow and
drift

Sunday the 7th wind N^{o} W^{t}.
hard gales and drift fine
weath^{r}. in ye afternoon

Munday the 8th fresh gales
Ditto clear and drift 12 of
our went to cut next winters
fireing at ten shilling creek
the rest of our hands cleaned y^{e}
house & platform of snow

[75]

Tuesday the 9th moderate gales
N^{o}. W^{t} clear weather our men

worked ye same the mohawk went
a hunting kill'd 1 patridge

Wednesday the 10th little wind
clear & sharp our men at home went
a wooding & one man came from ten
shilling creek to grind broken hatchets

Thursday ye 11th wind W^{t}. weather
ditto our men worked ditto & ye man
returned to ten shilling creek y^{e} mohawk
went a hunting did not return at night
we supposed he is gone to look for y^{e} deer
hunters

Friday y^{e} 12th little wind between y^{e}
S^{o} & y^{e} E^{t}. cloudy to day our men did y^{e}
same and y^{e} mohawk return'd brought 3
patridges hard gales in y^{e} $Even^{g}$. snow &
drift &c

Saturday y^{e} 13th wind variable from y^{e} S^{o}
E^{t} to y^{e} N^{o}: W^{t}. W^{t}.erly some of our men
came from tenshilling creek for provision
our hunters kill'd 7 patridges

Sunday y^{e} 14th wind from west to north
$weath^{r}$. ditto

[76]

Munday y^{e} 15th fresh gales at N^{o} E^{t}. w^{th}
snow y^{e} men returned to ten shilling
creek our men at home pull'd down y^{e}
Crest work y^{e} french had put upon y^{e}
cook r^{o}om &c

Tuesday y^{e} 16th wind & $weath^{r}$. Ditto &c

Wednesday y^{e} 17th wind & $weath^{r}$. y^{e} same

Thursday y^{e} 18th little wind E^{st}. wth snow till
noon it cleared ~~up~~ our men hove y^{e} snow
of y^{e} flankers.

Friday y^{e} 19th small winds E^{t}.erly clear
$weath^{r}$. our men went a wooding in y^{e}
plantation y^{e} mohawk & indian boy went a
hunting kill'd 13 patridges to day whiskers
went from y^{e} fort with his family &c

Saturday y^{e} 20th wind ditto & thaw
this day our men returned from
cutting y^{e} next winters wood our
hunters kill'd 12 patridges our men at
home clean ye platform

Sunday ye 21st small wind ye same
thaughed to day 3 indians came
from M^{r}. kelsey they having kill'd
no deer as yet but brought some dryed

flesh four moose tongues & 3 noses ditto &c

[77]

Monday ye 22^{d} wind & weath^{r}. ditto ye 3 indians & ye old womans boy return'd ye gov^{r}: began to overhaul ye stores our hunters kill'd 9 patridges &c

Tuesday ye 23^{d} wind & weath^{r}. ye same our people continue to work in ye ware house ye mohawk kill'd 4 patridges &c

Wednesday ye 24th wind ditto wth snow our men went to woods in ye morn^{g}. in ye aftern^{n}. got ye great morter of ye platform to ye E^{t}. end of ye Gov^{rs}. house without ye fortification to day came in four indians from ye S^{o}.ward

Thursday ye 25th strong gales N^{o}.therly wth small snow & drift ye indians presented ye gov^{r}. wth some tongues heads & flesh & traded some skins at Even^{g}. left ye fort our hunters kill'd 12 patridges 2 strang~~ers~~ indians came in from M^{r} kelsey no deer as yet

Friday ye 26th moderate gales between ye N^{o}. & ye E^{t}. cloudy this day ye Indians wife & ye french Capt^{s}. son came to ye fort to day ye Indians traded he his son & wife went away ye french Cap^{ts}. son & wife went to lye at their tent 13 patridges killd to day

[78]

Saturday ye 27th fresh gales S^{o}therly to day ye Govr. turn'd ye french cap^{ts}. son & wife from ye fort but they went & lay at ye tent in ye woods not following ye other indians & 8 patridges kill'd &c

Sunday ye 28th wind & weath^{r}. ditto thawing

Munday ye 29th variable winds for ye most part Est.erly thawy to day our men went to woods our hunters kill'd 29 patridges snowed this morn^{g}.

Tuesday ye 30th thick weath^{r}. wind N^{o}therly to day I came to ye fort brought 20 Deers tongues & & deer sides there being no Deer those Indians I had seen being 5 tents came to ye factory also this Even^{g}.

fired the great morter twice
our hunters kill'd 31 patridges
&c Batt Entertain'd

Wednesday ye 31st wind variable
small snow our men went to woods
& our hunters kill'd 7 patridges Rich^{d}.
stanton broke his gun &c

[79]

Thursday ~~y~~ april ye 1st wind and ~~weath~~
weath^{r}. ditto to day digged 2 barrels of
beer out buried last fall made a feast
for the indians told them they must
goe out of our way y^{t} our people might
hunt which they agreed too our hunt
ers kill'd 30 patridges

Friday the 2^{d} wind and weather
ditto our hunters kill'd 19 patridges
fired one of the Brass pieces 3 times
one tent of the Indians went over the
river pointed some palasadoes to
day &c

Saturday the 3^{d} fine weather wind
S^{o}therly thawed our hunters kill'd 84
patridges and 2 Rabbits some of the
indians went away likewise 3 came
from those indians to the Southward
which say there is no deer &c

Sunday the 4th strong gales at
N^{o}.E^{t}. close weather more indians
went away and having left but
one tent which removed into the
plantation &c

[80]

Munday the 5th wind N^{o} E^{t}. with
snow sleet and rain thawed much
the 3 indians that came a
saturday last went away and
another with them

Tuesday the 6^{t} much snow
last night wind N^{o}.therly our
hunters kill'd 55 patridges and
one indian came from the
fourteens brought 8 rabbits traded
them for 5 pints of oatmeal
turn'd one indians out of the
fort

Wednesday the 7th wind ditto
with small snow our hunters
kill'd 82 patridges and 11

rabbits and the indian~~s~~ return'd
to his tent at the fourteens

Thursday the 8th strong
gales ditto clear our hunters
kill'd 57 patridges

friday the 9th fine weath^{r} wind S^{o}therly
thawed our hunters killd 59
patridges and one rabbit one indian &
his wife came to ye fort from up the river who
says there is no deer

[81]

Saturday the 10th wind and weather ditto
our hunters kill'd 78 patridges those
at home hove snow out of the yard to
day came 2 indians from the Islands
that brou∧^{gh}t 6 rabbits so traded and
went away

Sunday the 11th wind and weath^{r}.
ditto 2 indians came in from the
south side of the river one of which
traded and went away the other
stayed here thawed very much
to day

Munday the 12th fine weath^{r}.
wind N^{o}therly small frost last
night to day came 7 indians from
the south shore who traded and
went away gave us acco^{t}. some deer
had past yesterday another said
he saw two geese our hunters
kill'd 11 patridges clear'd the
platform of water

[82]

Tuesday the 13th wind and weather
variable our hunters kill'd 10 patridges
clear'd part of the trading room
here came tents of indians to y^{e}
fort

Wednesday the 14th thick
weather ∧$^{wind\ variable}$ this morning made an
end clearing the trading room
and ~~told~~ delivered into y^{e} warehouse
whole parchment beaver 158
coat ditto 208 half ditto 110
otter 10 and muse skins 9 receivd
some goods into y^{e} trading room
&c told into the warehouse 38
coat beaver 26 half and 12 whole
parchment fired the morter
twice

Thursday the 15th cold snowy
Blowing weather wind $N^{o}E^{t}$.
to day our people went to carry
y^{e} things over y^{e} river for goose hunting
Likewise to carry y^{e} sawed plank to y^{e}
fourteen house

[83]

friday the 16th Clear weath^{r} wind
N^{o}therly to day our people returned from
the other side having help the goose
hunters to their place and removed
the plank the indians likewise traded
to day 3 patridges kill'd and 3 hundred
of musket shott cast into pistol
buttertooth kept

Saturday the 17th wind and weath^{r}.
ditto some of the indians went away
and our indian~~s~~ returned from
up the river who says he saw
some geese but no deer one hand
came from the goose tent for
provision 6 patridges kill'd to day
and one Rabbit our men Clipt shot
for trading

Sunday the 18th wind W^{t}.erly
cold more indians went away
guyers clild went from the factory

Munday ye 19th moderate weath^{r}. wind N^{o}.
W^{t}. our men went to woods for fireing some
indians went away to ye south side & our
hunters killd 24 patridges & said saw one goose

[84]

Tuesday the 20th fair weather wind
ditto thawed a little our men
continue wooding sawed some
board att the fort our hunters kill'd
19 patridges

Wednesday the 21st thawy
wind E^{t}erly one hand went to
the goose tent one ye south side
the ramaing part of those indians
that came from the southward
went away from the fort and
in the evening our hand returned
brought 24 patridges run more
shott our hunters kill'd ~~kill'd~~ 10
patridges

Thursday the 22^{d} wind
and weather ditto our men work
heaving the snow out of the garden

and some a cliping the shott some
more indians went away our
hunters kill'd 24 patridges

[85]

Friday the 23^{d} Clear wind S^{o}therly
much thaw our men made an end
of clearing the garden the remaining
part of the indians went away
except those belonged to the fort
one English and one mohawk
came from the tent on the other
side brought 91 patridges fired
the morter twice this even^{g}. one break
factory went away also

Saturday the 24th wind and
weath^{r}. ditto to day gott six ~~minnion~~
minnion guns of the flankers
our man returned to his tent saw four
geese one tent of Indians came starv'd
from the south side

Sunday the 25th fair weath^{r}.
wind ditto saw several geese the
Indians went a hunting one of ~~whi~~
which killd 4 & brought y^{m} to y^{e}
Govern^{r}. traded 3 of y^{m} for oatmeal

[86]

Munday the 26th fog, this morn^{g}.
till nine it cleared & thawed
much our hunters kill'd 2 geese
one of which kitt spencer killd
and one indian came from the
tent on the south side who
say'd they had kill'd no geese
but had 4 which indians kil'd
Likewise another indian and
his wife came from this side of
portnelson saying he has
seen no geese yet our people at
home went to woods removed
the plank and hove away
the snow from the N^{o} E^{t} corner
of the$^{Gov.rs}$house toward Evening
it rain'd wind N^{o} E^{t}. strong
gales

Tuesday the 27th wind ditto frost
last night & snowed to day one indian
came from y^{e} french creek return'd in
the Even^{g}. to his tent our men hove y^{e}
snow from about y^{e} pinnace

[87]

Wednesday the 28th wind and weath^{r}. ditto the tent of Indians that was in the plantation went away to go up the river to hunt geese for a night or two but finding the river broak up aloft returned Likewise another tent which was on the south side of portnelson came hither having seen no geese and the Indian wch came from our people on the south shore returned

Thursday the 29th thick weath^{r}. wind ditto went a hunting had no success our men at home work a doubling the E^{t}. side of the cook room one indian came from the south side ye river out of ye plains who says there is many geese and brough 4 with him 4 of our men went into the marsh with a tent

Friday the 30th weath^{r}. clear wind ditto this morn^{g}. Mr Bishop came to the fort brought nothing by reason of bad weath^{r} we continue about the cook room ye indian return'd y^{t} brought ye 4 geese & 2 more wth him

[88]

Saturday the 1st of may this morn^{g}. M^{r}. Bishop returned being fine weather little wind S^{o}.therly went a hunting kill'd one goose also came one hand from the tent in the marsh for provision they having but few geese our people continue about the cook room

Sunday the 2^{d} snowed last night continues the same to day with strong gales at N^{o}. E^{t}erly one of our indians went over the river yesterday Even^{g}. to lye there likewise those belonging to the tents in the plantation returned from ye other side brought 2 geese

Munday the 3^{d} wind & weath^{r}. ditto till ten this morn^{g}. clearing up & strong gales at E^{t}. our indian returned from tother side no success went a hunting but

no game but batt kill'd 9 patridges & 1 Rabbit
our man likewise return'd to ye tent
in the marsh our men hove ye snow of y^{e}
flankers & out of the yard

[89]

Tuesday the 4th rain'd har'd last night
wind S^{o}therly cleared this morning went
ahunting kill'd 9 Geese had storms for
this 2 days past

Wednesday the 5 little wind variable
went a hunting no game one hand
went to ye tent in the marsh brought
one goose

Thursday the 6th fair weath^{r}. wind ditto
went a hunting kill'd 2 geese sent one
hand to the tent on the south side
but the creeks running came back
Mr Newton came from y^{t} tent brought
10 geese

friday the 7th Cloudy fresh gales
S^{o}therly went a hunting kill'd 12 geese
our man return'd to the tent on tother
side and some indians that was at ye french
creek came over with their tents to y^{e}
fort

Saturday y^{e} 8th clear wind ditto went a hunting
kill'd 10 geese one indian came from y^{e} french
creek brought 11 geese who return'd in y^{e} Even^{g}. to
day was finished a frame for a cook room &
smith shop

[90]

Sunday the 9th wind from the E^{t} to
S^{o}E^{t} fine weath^{r}. $_{\wedge}$^{with} some rain in the
Evening 2 hands with one mohawk
came from the goose tent on the S^{o}
side this morning brought 39 geese
likewise 1 hand from the tent in the
marsh brought 1 ditto our hunters
kill'd 7 geese & some

Munday the 10th wind & weath^{r}
variable went a hunting killd 2
geese and some ducks our people
repact the salt meat and the men
return'd to their tent in the marsh
took our 2 indians with him and
the carpenters a refitting the
boats

Tuesday the 11th Cloudy wind N^{o}. E^{t}.
went a hunting kill'd one goose

& some ducks the carpenters
remain doing the boats

Wednesday the 12th one hand came from
ye tent in ye marsh brought 3 geese & 1 swan
ye carpenters ~~are working~~‸continue to work upon ye boats y^{e}
hunters kill'd 2 geese & some ducks wind
E^{t}erly clear weath^{r}.

[91]

Thursday the 13th wind S^{o}therly
weather ditto the hand return'd to the
tent this morn^{g}. our carpenters are working
upon the boats about 2 afternoon one hand
came from ye tent in ye marsh who brought
6 geese & a Gun to be mended wch being done
he returned to the tent our hunters kill'd
7 geese this night Mr Kelsey & M^{r} spencer
lay at the tent in ye marsh ~~till y^{e}~~
& to lye out till ye govern^{r}. made a signal
for their return

Friday ye 14th an indian traded 4
geese wth the gov^{r}. for powder & shott one
hand came from the goose tent in ye marsh
for powder & shott he brought 4 geese
he return'd to ye tent at again our
hunters kill'd 18 geese one swan &
some ducks likewise 3 hands went
from the fort to ye tent at marsh
& brought from thence 18 geese our
Carpenters are working upon ye boats
little wind E^{t}erly wth rain in ye aftern^{n}.

[92]

Saturday the 15th wind N^{o}therly thick
weath^{r}. our carpenters a fixing ye boats
& making Oars our hunters kill'd 5
geese & 1 duck some hands went to y^{e}
tent in ye marsh & brought from thence
13 geese some indians came from ye S^{o}
side one of wch traded 13 geese wth ye govern^{r}
for powder & shott one hand came from
ye tent in ye marsh for flower

Sunday ye 16th hard gales E^{t}erly wth rain
hail thunder & snow this morn^{g}. about
4 ye river broke up

Munday ye 17th little winds N^{o}therly clear
weath^{r}. in ye aftern^{n}. ye hand y^{t} came for
flower returned to ye tent ye indian y^{t}
traded ye geese on saturday Inform'd y^{e}
gov^{r}. y^{t} there was some carpenters tools in
a boat wch was upon the South side
wch we suppose to be the deerings long

boat which drove from the ship in
bad weath^{r}. so the gov^{r}. sent 2 hands
in the yaul & the indian but they
could not come near the boat for ice

[93]

the yaul returned wth the 2 hands &
brought 2 corking irons a hamer & auger
which they had from the indians tent
which he gott out of her before this
Evening 4 cannoes of indians came
down the river to the fort upon w^{ch}
the governer made the signal for
M^{r} kelsey's return to the fort who
returned to with another hand that
came for powder & shott

Tuesday the 18th fresh gales N^{o} E^{t}. sent
four hands to the tent in ye marsh who
brought from thence forty geese traded
with those indians that came
yesterday

Wednesday the 19th wind & weath^{r}.
ditto this morning gott some timber to
the E^{t} End of the governers house &
some hands went into the marsh
who returned with small game told
beav^{r}. into ye warehouse

[94]

Thursday the 20th fair weath^{r} wind
ditto this morning came six cannoes
which traded and went away about
noon in the Evening came an
indian from the french creek
brought 2 geese traded & went
away our hunters killd 6 geese
& some small fowls &c

Friday the 21st wind and weath^{r}
ditto this morning the four cannoes
that came first went away I and 3
~~I and 3~~ hands went with a boat
to ten shilling creek another boat
went likewise to the tent on the
South side and 2 hand went
into the marsh to fetch geese
brought 20 we gott four
trout our hunters kill'd
one goose and some small
fowls

[95]

Saturday the 22^{d} fair weather wind
ditto went again to ten shilling

creek caught nine fish our boat
return'd from tother side brought
80 geese and one of their hands
for things they want who says
they have about four hundred
geese at their tent our hunters
kill'd 2 geese

Sunday the 23^{d} fresh gales at
S^{o} E^{t} one hand came from the
tent in the marsh brought 1
goose the indians brought 15
geese and traded

Munday the 24th fine weath^{r}.
little wind S^{o}therly one boat
went to the S^{o} side with our
man which came from thence
and another went to ten shilling
creek wch brought some fish three
cannoes came down this afternoon who
says there is more ~~a~~ coming our boat came
from tother side & a cannoe wth 3 indians who ~~brought~~
brought from our tent 25 geese likewise 25 geese
Likewise 24 from our marsh &c lancht our boats
afloat told beaver into the warehouse

[96]

Tuesday the 25th thick weath^{r}.
wind N^{o}therly this morning the
indians traded and went away &
one cannoe came to the fort our
boat went to ten shilling creek
caught some fish to day pull'd
down part of the palasadoes on
the E^{t}. side of the governer's
house and batt came from
the tent in the marsh who
says but few geese there
Likewise some indians from
tother side$_{\wedge}$^{that} says the same
told beaver into the warehouse

Wednesday the 26 rainy weath^{r}.
wind S^{o}therly the cannoe that
came yesterday traded this
morning began to raise a work
on the W^{t}. side of y^{e} gov^{rs}. house bat
returned to y^{e} tent in y^{e} marsh

[97]

Thursday the 27th fine weath^{r}.
till about noon wind came E^{t}erly
with rain two boats went to the
goose tent on the south side
return'd in the Evening brought

125 geese I likewise went to ten
shilling creek caught some fish
one hand came from the tent
in the marsh and says the geese
are gone work'd to day fortification
the S^{o} side of the Governers house
the cannoe that traded
yesterday went away

Friday the 28th fresh gales ~~at~~
E^{t}erly with fog and rain 19 cannoes
came to the fort our 2 boats went again
to tother side to fetch the men ~~the~~ &
their things Likewise our hunters
came home from the marsh continue
to on the Gov^{rs}. house

[98]

Saturday the 29th snowed hard wind
ditto traded those cannoes that came
yesterday 18 more came to day & our
boats return'd from tother side &
brought all the men & 19 geese

Sunday the 30th fresh gales S^{o}therly
Cloudy with rain traded those indians
that came yesterday 21 cannoes
to day

Munday the 31st wind N^{o} E^{t} Cloudy
our carpenters & hands continue
working upon the governers house
to day 3 cannoes came to the fort
and some sayled having traded
told Beaver into the warehouse

Tuesday the 1st June wind
S^{o}therly with some rain about 16
or 17 cannoes came to day
likewise I traded those came
yesterday part of wch went away

[99]

Wednesday June the 2^{d} thick
weath^{r}. wind N^{o}therly the indians
that came yesterday traded &
went away 3 of our indians sent
over the river to hunt deer gott 2
guns mounted in the governers
house & took up part of the platform
being decayed told Beaver into the
warehouse

Thursday the 3^{d} wind E^{t}erly fresh
gales to day pull'd down the breast
work of the E^{t} and south flankers &
laid part of the platform several

cannoes came down this afternoon
amongst which came one of the
french men

friday the 4th strong gales S^{o}therly
with rain here came a large fleet
of cannoes to the fort likewise a
small parcel came from portnelson
by land traded some to day our men
took up more of the platform
being defective

[100]

Saturday the 5th fair $weath^{r}$
wind S^{o}therly ~~with rain here~~ ^ some cannoes came to day
our people made an end of the
platform & gott our guns in their
places we have now about 50
cannoes at the fort

Sunday the 6 wind N^{o}therly
weather ditto some came to day
& others went away our frenchman
and bat went up the river to
hunt deer

Munday the 7th fair $weath^{r}$.
wind ditto some cannoes
came to day & others went
away we begun to lay the
foundation of a platform
at the East end of the
Governers house and some
hands went to the
fourteens to gett the plank
down the river

[101]

Tuesday the 8th some rain and
snow last night ~~came to day~~ wind Notherly
fair weather to day some cannoes
came to day traded all the rest
and told the Beaver out of the
trading room into the warehouse
melted more small shott to make
caliver

Wednesday the 9th rainy $weath^{r}$.
wind S^{o}therly about 20 cannoes
came to day and some went
away

Thursday the 10th thick $weath^{r}$.
wind N^{o}therly all the indians
traded and went away 27 cannoes
of stone indians came this
Evening

Friday the 11th wind & weath^{r}.
Ditto to day came 14 cannoes
likewise 3 indians from tother
side we gott the 2 guns of the
lower platform up on the new
platform at the E^{t} end of the

[102]

Saturday the 12 clear weather wind
N^{o}~~therly~~ W^{t}. our people returned from
the fourteens having gott the plank
to the rivers mouth to day the stone
Indians traded and went away four
cannoes came down the river and
some indians from portnelson
cast more shott

Sunday the 13th wind and weath^{r}.
ditto traded to day part of the
Indians went away others stayed
for want of caliver shott

Munday the 14th Clear wind
E^{t}erly 3 boats went to the fourteens
to fetch boards and to secure the
albemarle with an anchor and
hasser which they carryed with
them one boat came with a raft
to the rivers mouth and to the
fort in the night all the Indians
traded & went away four cannoes
came to day told the beaver out of
ye trading room into ye warehouse

[103]

Tuesday the 15th wind and weath^{r}.
ditto our tother boat came to the fort
about noon with the quantitie of boards
being sixty eight two cannoes came to
day traded and went away at Ebb our
pinnice went for the remainer of the
boards one cannoe came down this
Evening

Wednesday the 16th wind and
weather the same the indians traded
and went away Likewise an indian
came from tother side we begun to
raise the Bullwark of the platform
at the East end of the Governers house
some indians came from portnelson
saying they are 19 cannoes all of stone
indians

Thursday the 17th fair weather
wind variable to day came the

french man from tother side brought
some fish Likewise some indians
with deers flesh and the indians
that came down portnelson came
all to the fort & traded part of
their Beaver last night our pinnace

[104]

return'd with the rest of the
plank

friday the 18th wind E^{t}erly
weath^{r}. ditto to day came 3
cannoes to the for with deers
flesh best part of those indians
that had traded went away our
people set up palasadoes to secure
the bank and the french man
went over the river to fish & hunt
Likewise those indians that
came from tother side went over
with them

Saturday the 19th fine weath^{r}.
wind S^{o}therly traded the deers
flesh that came yesterday four
cannoes came to day that went
from hence 2 days ago continue
securing the bank and told
the Beaver into the
warehouse

[105]

Sunday the 20th wind S^{o}therly
some rain this morning the french
man came over brought some fish
and fowl likewise came 3 cannoes of
Indians that went from hence
sometime since having seen no
deer and those indians stayed
behind the rest went away this
morning being six cannoes

Munday the 21st fair weath^{r}.
wind E^{t}erly 2 boats went this
morning to ten shilling creek to
raft Likewise the frenchman
went over to the nets 2 cannoes
of indians came to the fort
from tother side brought nothing
our boats return'd at Evening
having made the rafts but
could gett them home
tide being spent

Torn out till July the 2^{d}

[106]

friday the 2^{d} wind S^{o}W hott weath^{r}
several indians came from the S^{o} side of
the river to the fort our Carpenters
and hands are working as yesterday

Saturday the 3^{d} fair weath^{r}. wind
between the N^{o} and E^{t} small gales
I returned to the fort about 4 this
~~Evening~~ afternoon gott to the
seafords pinnace yesterday about
the same time corkt her and launcht
her being about 45 miles from
the fort came away this morn^{g}.
about four a clock some plain
indians arrived att the fort
since I went away and remain
here still

Sunday the 4th much rain
last night with strong gales
variable from the S W to the N^{o}
E^{t} the indians brought some
deers flesh and tongues & had
given ye Govr. 2 young foxes & one
young martin

[107]

Munday the 5th fresh gales at N^{o} E^{t}
sent 2 boats to the albemarle to see
to get her of continue at home to pack
beaver and fill cannon baskets & to
secure the bank

Tuesday the 6th moderate gales
variable 2 hands came from ye abbemarle
who went to help them with the boats
& brought news of a white whale drove
a shore which I ~~brought~~ shott last
saturday comeing up with ye seafords
pinnice our people continue to work
as formerly & ye gov^{r}. went with y^{e}
yaul to sound ye channels

Wednesday ye 7th small winds N^{o}
therly I went with our pinnace to
fetch ye whale one indian came
from portnelson brought 2 young
foxes & some tongues bat went
away to day with indians upon
acco^{t}. of making a peace wth his
country people ye wch we incouraged as
much as possible much rain to day return'd
at even to ~~his~~ ye fort

[108]

Thursday ye 8th wind & weath^{r}. ditto
dryed up ye whale & continue to work
as formerly the carpenters raising
the uper work of the cook
room

Friday the 9th fair weath^{r}. wind
E^{t}erly to day ye gov^{r}. went at high
water wth ye yoall to ye albemarle
in hopes to get her of continue at
home to work as ₱ yesterday
&c /

Saturday the 10th fair weath^{r}
wind ditto this afternoon the
Governer came home said had
moved the albemarle a small
matter but could not gett her off
continue to work as formerly about
the fort

Sunday the 11th last night much
rain wind between the S^{o}. & y^{e} W^{t}
& so about to y^{e} N^{o} E^{t} this morn^{g}.
& cleared up

[109]

Munday the 12th cloudy wind E^{t}erly wth
rain this morn^{g}. went to y^{e} albemarle
with a cannoe they having hove
her off about her leng$_{\wedge}^{t}$h~~t~~ returned in
y^{e} aftern^{n}. they having workt at
home a putting of pieces of old
boats & filling y^{m} wth stones to secure
y^{e} banks & pulling down y^{e} chimney
y^{e} Gov^{rs}. house & y^{e} french man went
up y^{e} river to see if deer crost

Tuesday y^{e} 13th wind & weath^{r}. ditto set
up palasadoes to secure ye bank y^{e}
carpenters continue to work as ~~formerl~~
formerly

Wednesday ye 14th wind W^{t}erly clear this
morn^{g}. workt as yesterday till
about noon sent our pinnace to
ten shilling creek for a raft & I went
over ye river to a smoak wch proved to be
Indians who said our people were
coming from ye albemarle by land
so stay'd & brought 4 of y^{m} in ye cannoe
to ye fort in ye even^{g}. &c said they had
hove ye vessel of 3/4 of a cable &c

[110]

Thursday ye 15th wind & weath^{r}. ditto more

Indians came over to day one of wch inform'd ~~us~~ ye Govr. of a boat half way between this & severn upon wch I & 9 hands wth ye indian set out to fetch her in a Shallop our hands return'd wth a raft from tenshilling creek our carpenters & hands working as formerly

Friday ye 16th wind E^{t}erly weath^{r} ditto ye indians Traded some dryed flesh & tongues ye boy Jack & tom ye mohawk went to ye nets at ye fourteen river & brought some fish work ditto

Saturday ye 17th wind W^{t}erly weath^{r}. hott ye boy Jack & Tom ye mohawk went to ye nets again brought some fish & small fowl our hands work ditto likewise 2 indians brought 100 or 200 small fowl

Sunday ye 18th wind & weath^{r}. ditto thunder light ning & rain last night and some to day

Munday ye 19th wind E^{t}erly moderate weath^{r}. some hands went over to ye S^{o} shore to raft some drift wood but return'd without it they having not made it near Enough to low water mark so y^{t} it did not float at high water our hands are working upon ye Palasadoes & our carpenters as formerly

[111]

Tuesday ye 20th winds S W hot weath^{r}. some hands went again to ye S^{o} shore to raft more drift wood wch they brought at high water 2 hands went to lye out in ye marsh to look out for ships ye rest workt as yesterday fired the great morter twice

Wednesday ye 21st little winds W^{t}erly weath^{r}. ditto this even^{g}. saw 2 vessels in ye offin wch we could not make so prepared for an enemy & divided our hand into 3 watches

Thursday ye 22^{d} wind N^{o} E^{t} wth fog this morn^{g}. gott to ye fort wth ye long boat & shallop found ye long boat about 33 leagues from hence being ye same ye hudsons bay lost years since & little ye worse upon my arrival some hands went to ye albemarle to get her off y^{e} indian y^{t} went wth me for y^{e} boat is entertaind in y^{e} fort to hunt

Friday y^{e} 23^{d} wind S^{o}therly wth rain our boat went to y^{e} french creek for a raft our carpenters work as formerly some of y^{e} indians went away ~~at high~~ for portnelson ~~at high~~‸ $^{\text{our boat}}$ return'd at high water wth y^{e} raft

Saturday y^{e} 24th wind N^{o}therly a hard gale thick weath^{r}. to day y^{e} french man return'd from up y^{e} river by himself brought wth him some fresh deers flesh & a young live deer wch died soon after by reason being tyed so long in y^{e}

cannoe 2 hands likewise came from ye albemarle saying they had gott her a good distance of & had broke their anchor so sent another away immediately & ye indians y^{t} were about ye house went away up ye river &c

[112]

Sunday ye 25th wind between y^{e} N^{o}. & y^{e} W^{t}. fresh gales this morn^{g}. I went aboard y^{e} ship wth our pinnace at ¾ flood floated & stood of when had 2 fathom water came away wth y^{e} boat to y^{e} fort y^{e} ship at high water came to anchor in y^{e} mouth of y^{e} river & about 6 this Even^{g}. ^$^{weighed\ \&}$gott to y^{e} fort about 9

Munday y^{e} 26th wind W^{t}erly fair weath^{r}. to day repaired y^{e} slip & secured y^{e} bank y^{e} french man went up y^{e} river to see for more deer & one hand came from y^{e} tent in y^{e} marsh brought some small fowls at ~~Even~~ Even^{g}. y^{e} wind came E^{t}erly & blowed fresh

Tuesday ye 27th little wind variable fine weath^{r}. to day brought 2 long boats of stones to secure ye bank ye carpenters continue to work as formerly

Wednesday ye 28th wind & weath^{r}. D^{o} our cannoe return'd from ye french creek brought some fish & fowl our boats continue to fetch stones in ye even^{g}. 2 cannoes came down ye river wth deers flesh ye wch I traded & our yaul went to tenshilling creek for charcoal 2 cannoes went over ye river to fish & hunt sett one net at ye point of ye marsh

Thursday ye 29th wind & weath^{r}. D^{o} ~~to~~^^{this} ~~day~~ morn^{g}. four a clock came one cannoe from up ye river wth deers flesh traded it & all 3 went away together our boats went gathering of stones to do as formerly some hands a hunting kill'd small fowls heard a noise like a great gun at 11 a clock

Friday ye 30th wind N^{o}therly squally weath^{r}. continue to fetch stones our carpenters work as formerly & ye 2 cannoes return'd from tother side brought some small fowl some hands hunted in marsh did ye same

Saturday ye 31st wind & weath^{r}. D^{o}. today pulld down ye E^{t} flanker y^{t} Joyned to ye warehouse likewise took part of ye powder out of ye powder room it being moist without side to sort it out hunters kill'd some small fowl this evening came an Indian girl to ye fort who said there was a woman coming also

[113]

Sunday august ye 1st fair weath^{r} wind W^{t}erly our indian went a hunting but had no success ye woman I mentioned yesterday came here to day being left behind by those y^{t} went over portnelson & almost starved ye Govr. gave her a quart of ~~oatmea~~ oatmeal & at Even^{g}. wind came about E^{t}erly hawld ye albemarle ashore to dry at low water

Munday ye 2^{d} Cloudy a strong gales at E^{t}. this morn^{g}: gott y^{e}

powder into ye trading room & stowed it in ye beav^{r}. wth 2 bundles all round it & 4 bundles on ye top & gott our muskets all loaded & put in ye armoury wch is on ye top of ye Gov^{rs}. house where ye chimney was pull'd down took up some of ye platform before ye door of ye same house to new lay it & 2 hands went a hunting kill'd some small fowl one hand came from y^{e} look out tent brought some likewise made wads for y^{e} great guns

Tuesday y^{e} 3^{d} fair weath^{r}. wind variable from W^{t}. to y^{e} E^{t}. N^{o}therly to day fetcht 4 boats of stones ******* ~~went~~ ‸$^{\text{to secure ye bank}}$& unhung y^{e} albemarles ruther to mend it likewise kept a day watch of one hand on y^{e} house & laid part of y^{e} platform by y^{e} great gate 2 hands went a hunting ~~in y^{e} marsh~~ killd some small fowl &c burt match all night

Wednesday y^{e} 4th wind between y^{e} S & y^{e} E^{t}hazzy to day fetcht 4 boats of stones & 2 cannoes went over ye river one hand a hunting in ye marsh had small game one of y^{m} came from ye tent wth a broken gun gott another & return'd our carpenters made an end of laying ye platform one of y^{m} to making a new ruther for ye albemarle of plank ye old one being of no use

Thursday ye 5th storm gales at E^{t}. wth much rain our carpent ers work in ye Gov^{rs}. house this Even^{g}. one cannoe return'd from tother side brought home ye nets & 5 ducks

friday ye 6th fair weath^{r}. little wind E^{t}erly this morn^{g}. put up orders of quartering ye men & fetcht 2 boats of stones one hand went hunting in ye marsh brought some fish & fowl to day pact some beaver

Saturday ye 7th wind & weath^{r}. ditto to day fetcht 2 boats of stones & pulld down ye ye french battery pact ye rest of ye beav^{r}. our hunters killd some small fowl in ye Even^{g}. our indian returnd from tother side brought best part of a deer & about 2 dozzen of ducks

Sunday ye 8th wind between ye N^{o} & ye E^{t}. moderate gales clear one hand y^{t} came from ye tent in ye marsh yesterday return'd this morn^{g}. & one hand went to ye nets in ye marsh brought some fish & small fowl

Munday ye 9th fine weath^{r}. wind ditto to day 11 a clock‸^{sent}3 boats a rafting wth seven men in each our carpenters cut out loop holes in ye N^{o}. & W^{t}. flankers & mended ye steps Gov^{rs}. slip our hunters kill'd some small fowl

[114]

Tuesday ye 10th this morn^{g}. at 3 our boats return'd having brought their rafts to ye Creeks mouth & went for ye rafts & brought y^{m} to ye fort at 3 in ye even^{g}. our carpenters work upon ye ruther our hunters kill'd some fowl & brought some fish

Wednesday ye 11th wind E^{t}erly fair weath^{r}. at 11 ye morn^{g}. our 3 boats went again a rafting to tenshilling creek a tent of plain indians y^{t} came munday last went hence to ye S^{o}ward to day our hunters kill'd some fowl & some fish caught in ye nets in ye marsh

Thursday ye 12th fine weath^{r}. wind between ye N^{o} & ye W^{t}. to day about noon I brought our rafts to ye creeks mouth so left y^{m} & came home wth ye boats & out hunters kill'd some ~~small~~ fowl & caught some fish

Friday ye 13th thick fog wind N^{o}.therly at noon went for our rafts at four this Even^{g}. gott y^{m} to ye fort one indian came ~~fro~~ from portnelson who says ye rest of his family is there being ye french Capt. our hunters kill'd some small fowl & one goose also some fish

Saturday ye 14th Cloudy wind S^{o}therly last night one of ye rafts broak away it being very thick I sent 2 hands wth a yaul but could not find it this morn^{g}. clear'd a little could see it from ye fort our people carryed 3 rafts up ye bank at high water fetcht ye raft y^{t} drove away last night our hunters kill'd some small fowl & one goose ye french man told me he found a dead man in ye marsh so sent 4 hands to see it proved to be Thos. Bullears boy & y^{t} died of ye rivers mouth last fall french Capt. came 3 cannoes

Sunday ye 15th fair weath^{r}. wind S^{o}therly one hand went to ye net caught some fish

Munday ye 16th little wind ditto this morn^{g}. 2 o Clock our 3 boats went to ten shilling creek to rafting & in ye Even^{g}. they all return'd two of y^{m} brought their rafts wth y^{m} ye other came aground being ye last of w^{t} was cut in ye spring

Tuesday ye 17th strong gales from ye E^{t} to ye N^{o}. wth rain this even^{g}. 8 a Clock saw a fire made at ye french Creek

Wednesday ye 18th fresh gales N^{o}therly to day carryed 3 rafts of wood up ye bank ye indians y^{t} made ye fire at ye french creek last night came to ye fort reporting they heard great guns a sunday last our hunters kill'd some fowl & ~~fish~~ caught some fish

Thursday ye 19th fair weath^{r}. wind S^{o}therly this morn^{g}. four a clock our 3 boats went up ye river a rafting wth 23 men to day all ye indians went over ye river & in ye aftern^{n}. we saw a smoak wch was to be a signal they saw ships our hunters kill'd some fowl & fish

[115]

friday ye 20th wind W^{t}erly weath^{r}. ditto this Even^{g}. 11 a clock our boats came down wth their rafts

Saturday ye 21st fresh gales N^{o}therly cloudy wth squalls of rain our hunters killd some small fowl & fish

Sunday ye 22^{d} clear wind more W^{t}terly one hand went to ye nett caught some fish fresh gales

Monday ye 23^{d} white frost wind S^{o} W^{t} clear this morn^{g}. four a clock Mr Bishop wth six hands went wth ye shallop to ye fourteens to lye out a goose hunting our men at home carryed 4 rafts of wood up ye bank

Tuesday ye 24th wind & weath^{r}. ditto our hands carryed up 2 rafts more they being ye last

Wednesday ye 25th wind W^{t}erly Blowing rainy weath^{r}. last night clear to day more hands went to lye out in our marsh in 2 tents a goose hunting & some hands went up ye river to make charcoal but seeing a ship at 10 in ye morn^{g}. all ye hands return'd home ye gov^{r}. sent me & eight hands to ye marsh to lye till we knew w^{t} ye ship was or untill further orders

Thursday ye 26th Clear weath^{r}. wind ditto this morn^{g} 4 a Clock our 2 pinnaces man'd went to see to make ye ship he hoisting a red Ensign at his maintopmast head but showed no other colours our boats returnd we seeing 3 ships more in the offin I sent one hand to ye fort to give ye gov^{r}. notice so came away wth ye shallop along wth ye pinnaces meeting ye hand I had sent who brought orders for him & 2 more to return to ye marsh & I wth ye others to go home had not been long there but saw a boat come from ye french creek so man'd ye 2 pinnaces went after her I likewise running down along shore she put back again our boats could not come up wth them it being almost high water & a fresh gale left their chase & return'd I also ~~****~~ meeting those 3 men y^{t} was in ye marsh who said they saw men landed in ye marsh so we return'd wth y^{m} all except one hand wch parted from y^{m} into ye woods when ye french boats was near this side who came home after us & ye ship wch rid of ye river wheiged & run of to sea after wch we heard several great guns at four afternoon M^{r} bishop wth 10 men more went to y^{e} point of y^{e} marsh to y^{e} shore

[116]

friday y^{e} 27th fresh gales N^{o}therly Cloudy this morn^{g}. 2 clock saw a cannoe at wch fired some muskets our people say'd they saw a fire at y^{e} back of y^{e} fort to day at 10 y^{e} ships weig$_{\wedge}^{h}$ed from y^{e} mouth of portnelson & stood for this river being only two at one a clock one came to anchor of our rivers mouth & fired 2 guns his boat came of from y^{e} fourteens & went aboard we fired one gun by consent for our men $_{\wedge}^{\text{to come}}$ home wch they did about five afternoon y^{e} other ship came to anchor of y^{e} point of y^{e} marsh to day broke up 2 chest of guns & loaded y^{m} & those remaining in y^{e} trading room in all about a hundred last night watcht 5 & 6 men in a watch 2 hours

Saturday y^{e} 28th fresh gales N^{o} E^{t}. last night watcht 10 in a watch 3 hours each about one this morn^{g}. our men said they saw men near ye palasadoes at wch they fired some small arms about noon it blowed very hard D^{o}. wth rain hail & snow in so much y^{t} ye albem arle drove & our deerings pinnace sunk at her

moorings ores & all things went a drift could not
launch a boat to fetch y^{m}

Sunday ye 29th fresh gale N^{o}therly this morn^{g}. half
foot snow on ye ground saw one of ye ships drove a
shore in ye marsh ye other not in sight our people
went down along shore to see for our pinnaces
ores found 6 of ye frenches ores & some rack att 11
forenoon man'd ye seafords pinnace Mr Bishop &
9 more in her went to look on ye ship but 2 boats
coming round ye point before he gott down they sent to
ye ship & fetcht more men so he lay a considerable
time afterwards returnd said they were loaden wth goods
his spritsail has been loose all day one hand came to y^{e}
woods Edge & fir'd 3 times at which we fired small arms

Munday ye 30th moderate gales between ye N^{o}. & ye W^{t}. frost
this morn^{g}. 5 a clock their boat went from ye place
where they landed there goods round to ye ships about 9
forenoon saw 3 ships more in sight at half Eb a boat
came from ye ships in ye offing to sheaground one
cannoe came down ye river

Tuesday ye 31st fair weath^{r}. wind ditto this morn^{g}. they landed
many men & came nearer ye fort at wch we fired several
great guns & ye great morter ~~twice~~ once about 9
forenoon a cannoe came from tother side wth cap^{t}.
smithson who gave an acco^{t}. of 16 or 18 men of his

[117]

on tother side so went wth a pinnace & 2 cannoes Mr Newton
in one & I in ye other in coming back Mr Newton was shott in
ye belly from ye woods Edge & kept fireing at their small
arms at ye fort & weat them now & then a great gun
rewarded ye Indians for Bringing cap^{t}: smithson traded y^{e}
others Beav^{r}. & sent y^{m} away watcht half watch this Even^{g}.
ye 2 ships came in to lower five fathom hole

Wednesday ye 1st Septr. fair weath^{r}. wind W^{t}erly
several small arms fired on both sides to day came
2 french men wth a flag of truce to demand ye 3 prison
ers wch we would not grant M^{r} newton dyed at 4 morn^{g}.

Thursday ye 2^{d} fine weath^{r}. small Breezes S^{o}W^{t} they
begun to play their morter hove 4 shells then
came wth a flag of truce to demand ye fort being denyed
went their way & fired again till they had hove 15
& we fourteen then came again telling us we
should have no quarters we told y^{m} if they would
not allow us time to consider we would have none
so ye Govr. drew up a paper & brought on ye platform
to satisfie ye men they should have every one a
years pay gratis if they would sign y^{e} ~~paper~~ ^same^ & we
kept ye fort some did signe others not & said would
not sell their lives for a little money so sent
our articles & in ye Even^{g}. I Mr Bishop Mr Clark
went to their camp to hear their final ans^{r} so

diberveal writt his resolution demanded ye fort
by one a clock ye next day & our answer by 8 in
ye morn^{g}.

friday ye 3^{d} fair weath^{r}. wind ditto finding such great force
as nine hundred men & ye ill tidings of our own ships
concluded could not keep it & so agreed to ye articles aforesign'd
by monseir & ye Govr. & marcht out by one a clock & ye french
took possession of ye fort this being ye end of a
Tedious winter & tragical Journal by
me Henry Kelsey

[118]

1698

A Journal of a Voyage by Gods permission
in ye deering frigott from England to hudsons
bay Ꝑ Capt crimmington Comm^{r}. &c In
1698 kept by me henry kelsey

Munday June ye 13th having sett our Pilot on shoar
this Even^{g}. & hoisted our Boats in 8 a Clock took our depart
ure from thorpness lying in ye latitude of 52^{d}: 30^{m} N^{o}
sent ye Perry a head went wth Easy sail till 8 this morn.
we went a head saw several sail about us this last 16
hours thick weath^{r}. wth some rain have made my course
N° 38^{d} : 8^{m} E^{t} diff: of latt^{d}. 60^{m} Dep^{tr}. 32^{m} : 8° Dist 68^{m} & at
12 noon had 15 fathom thorpness bore N.N W dist 3
mile

Tuesday June ye 14th Clear weath^{r}. wth moderate gales between
ye S^{o}W^{t} & W N W this afternoon spoke wth a ship called y^{e}
frienly society of London came from Norway soon after
took ye perry in a tow about midnight reeft maintopsail
this morn^{g}. fair weath^{r}. let out reef soundings att 2
this morn^{g}. 40 fath^{m}. at 4 : 18 at 6 : 20 at 8: 17 at 10 : 11 at
12 : 15 my diff Latt^{de}. 92^{m}'' 6° Dep^{tr}. 17^{m} : 2° Dist 93^{m} my true
course this 24 hours is N°. 05 : 37^{m} W^{t}.

Wednesday ye 15th Clear wth fine Breezes between ye S^{o}W
& N^{o}W^{t}. at 5 this Even^{g}. ye Perry lying a stern we lay by &
try'd for fish at 6 made sail soon after saw a dogger att
anchor right a head when we came up wth her our
pinnace went on board & bought some cods & ½ an
hour past 3 reeft both topsails & between ^{8} & 12 we
hand y^{m} both my diff of Latt^{de}. is 93^{m} Dep^{tr}. 55^{m}. dist
108^{m} my course made good this 24 hours is N°. 30^{d} : 56^{m} W^{t}
Thorpness bears of me this 16th day at noon S^{o}9^{d} : 35^{m}
E^{t} dist 248^{miles} I being in ye Latt^{de} of 56^{d} : 35^{m} N^{o}

Thursday ye 16th fresh gales from ye W^{t} to ye N^{o}W^{t} at 6 this
Even^{g}. set maintopsail & at half past 8 took it in again at
one after midnight hawl'd up foresail at 3 this morn^{g}. set him
again having laid a try 2 hours & at 6 this morn^{g}. set fore
topsail this morn^{g}. saw a dogger dist 4 miles my Diff of
latt^{de}. is 63^{m}. 2° Dep^{tr}. 42^{m}: 3° dist 76^{m} from ye 16 noon to ye 17th

noon my true course is N° 33^{d} : 45^{m} W^{t} [1]from thorpness bearing S^{o}308 miles I am in ye Latt^{de}. of 57^{d} : 38^{m} N^{o}.

[119]

friday ye 17th thick weath^{r}. wth moderate gales between N^{o}N^{o}W & W^{t}N^{o}W^{t}. at 6 this Even^{g}. set maintopsaile & 4 this morn^{g}. tackt & bore up to ye perry weath^{r}. very uncertain at forenoon took down our maintop gallant mast from ye 17th noon to ye 18th noon my diff Latt^{de} is 18^{m} 2° dep^{tr}. 11^{m} : 4° dist 21 ^{m} my true course ~~made good~~ is N° 33^{d} : 45^{m} W^{t}. thorness bears S^{o} 2^{d} : 49^{m} E^{t} Dist 330 miles I am in ye latt^{de} of 57^{d} : 56

Saturday ye 18th Clear wth Easy gales between ye N^{o}N^{o}W^{t} & S^{o}W^{t} this Even^{g}. at 6 very fair weath^{r} & at midnight tack & saw 12 or 13 sail of duch fishing busses sent our pinnace aboard they sent our cap^{t}. some cod then our boat went on board again wth a small present they sent us more cod & some herrings at 9 this forenoon tackt from ye 18th noon to ye 19th noon my course made good is W^{t} 32 miles diff latt^{de} oo thorpness bears S^{o} 8^{d} : 26^{m} E^{t} dist 333 miles I am in ye Latt^{d}. of 57^{d} : 56^{m}

Sunday ye 19th fair weath^{r}. little wind between ye W^{t} S^{o}therly at 4 this ~~mor~~*^{g}. aftern^{n}. went wth ye pinnace a fishing caught 3 cod Capt. Bayley came on board tarryed some time & returnd to his ship at 6 this morn^{g}. saw ye Land from ye 19th noon to ye 20th noon my course made good is W^{t} 8^{d} : 26^{m} N^{o} diff of Latt^{de} 12^{m} : 4° Dist 89^{m} thorpness bears S^{o} 22^{d}.30^{m} E^{t} dist 366 mile W^{t}ing 132 mile I am in ye Latt^{de} of 58^{d}.8^{m} N^{o}

Munday ye 20th fine gales between ye E^{t} & W^{t} S^{o}.therly at 3 this afternoon Dunkins head bore N^{o} N^{o} E Dist 3 leagues at 2 this morn^{g}. reeft topsails & at 4 came to an anchor in castin road in 6 fath^{m}. wind W^{t}. N^{o} W^{t} this 24 hours have had ye weath^{r}. very uncertain wth squall & rain

1 The "W" is indistinct.

[120]

month day	Latt^{de} P D D M D M	Easting in miles	W^{t}ing in miles	Course corrected from hoy head	Dist in m miles	West Longitude in D. miles	E^{t} Longitude in miles	variation	Course from day to day
Thursday June ye 23^{d}	59^{d}:36^{m}		75:2	N°13^{d} N°73^{d}:08^{m} W^{t}	79	15^{d}:50^{m}		16^{d}:52^{m}	N° 73^{d}:8^{m} W^{t}
friday June ye 24th to ye 25th noon	59:39		101	N° 78^{d}:45^{m} W^{t}	105	16^{d}:40^{m}		20^{d}:00	87:12 W^{t}
Saturday June ye 25th noon to ye 26th noon	60:03		133	N° 56^{d}:17^{m} W.^{t}	162	17^{d}:44^{m}		20:00	N.º 47^{d}:47^{m} W^{t}
from ye 26 noon to ye 27th noon	60:40		185	N° 64^{d}:43^{m} W^{t}	205	19:28			N° 56^{d}:15^{m} W^{t}
munday June ye 27th noon to ye 20th noon	60:03		222	N° 75^{d}:52^{m} W^{t}	228	20:42		20^{d}:30^{m}	S^{o} 45^{d}:00 W^{t}
Tuesday June ye 28th noon to ye 29th noon	58:43		284	S^{o} 84^{d}:23^{m} W^{t}	288	22:46			S^{o} 51^{d}:37^{m} W^{t}
Wednesday June ye 29th noon to ye 30th noon	58:49		332	S^{o} 87^{d}:13^{m} W^{t}	336	24:22			N° 81^{m}:32^{m} W^{t}
from ye 30th noon to ye 1 July ditto	57:49		378	S^{o} 75^{d}:58^{m} W^{t}	384	25:54			S^{o} 36^{d}:30^{m} W^{t}
from ye 1st noon to ye 2^{d} ditto	57:03		414	S^{o} 74^{d}:08^{m} W^{t}	438	27:06			S^{o} 39 W^{t}
from ye 2^{d} noon to ye 3^{d} Ditto	57:39		446	S^{o} 75^{d}:58^{m} W^{t}	462	28:10			N° 50^{d}:3^{m} W^{t}

[121]

Wednesday august ye 10th fresh gales between y^e *westing*
N^o E^t & S^o E^t E^{t}erly some times fog & rain we have *long miles*
sailed this 24 hours through shattered broken ledges
Latt^{de} of ice at noon saw a white Bear from ye 10th noon to
₽ D D ye 11th ditto my course made good is W^t 25^d : 17^m S^o diff *85 : 3^d: 07^m*
62^d : 34^m Latt^{de} 46^m : 01[1] Dep^{tr}. 98^m : 6° dist 111 miles & I find
cape diggs to bear of me E^t 21^d : 30^m N^o Dist 31 leagu^{es}

-D D Thursday y^e 11th fresh gales between y^e N^{o}W^t & y^e S^o E *110: 4^d : 02^m*
61^d : 48^m S^{o}therly about 6 this Even^g. gott clear w^{e}ath ^{r} foggy from
y^e 11th noon to y^e 12th ditto my course made good is S^o
25^d : 17^m W^t diff Latt^{de} 46$^{dm:}$ 3° dep^{tr} 25^m : 9° dist 53 miles
Digs bears E^t. 39^d : 38^m N^o Dist 46 Leagues

Latt^{de} ₽ D D Friday y^e 12th moderate gales from y^e S^o B E^t *153: 5^d: 51^m*
61^d : 00^m to y^e S^o W^t S^{o}therly weath^r. very uncertain my
course made is S^o 42^d : 13^m W^t diff Latt^{de} 48^n : 1°
dep^{tr}. 43^m : 0 dist 65 miles Digs bears E^t 39^d : 22^m N^o
dist 67 Leagues from ye 12th noon to ye 13th ditto

₽ D D Saturday ye 13th fine gales from ye S^o E to ye S^o W^t
59^d : 50^m S^{o}therly at this Even^g had an amplicate found y^e
variation to be 33^d : 15^m at 6 this morn^g. reeft both *183 : 6^d : 51^m*
topsails at 11 handed maintopsails at 12
handed foretopsails from ye 13th noon to ye 14th
ditto my course made good is S^o 22^d : 30^m W^t
diff Latt^{de} 70^m Dep^{tr}. 29^m : 8° dist 67 miles digs
bears N° 42^d : 13^m E^t Dist 91 Leagues

₽ D D Sunday ye 14th fresh gales from ye E^t S^o E^t to ye W^t *W^t ~~miles~~*
~~61^d : 00^m~~ S^o W^t S^{o}therly at 7 this Even^g. handed main *miles Long*
~~58^d : 50^m~~ topsails at 8 handed foretopsaile at 9 sett y^e
58^d : 48^m latter from ye 14th noon to ye 15th ditto my course *171 : 6^d: 28^m*
made good is S^o 11^d : 15^m E^t diff Latt^{de} 62^m : 4° dep^{tr}.
12^m : 9° dist 64 miles digs bears N° 33^d : 15^m E^t dist
104 Leagues *vari*
30 : 38

₽ observ Munday ye 15th hard gales from about S^o W^t
58^d : 20^m at 3 aftern^n handed foretopsail at 10 this *100 4^d : 15^m*
*~~**^{d}***~~* morn^g set both topsails sailing by a ledge of
broaken ice from ye 15th noon to ye 16th ditto my
course made good is E^t 22^d : 30^m S^o diff Latt^{de} 3 0^m
Dep^{tr} 70^m : 9° dist 78 miles digs bears N^o
~~bears N^o~~ 18^d : 50^m E^t dist 104 Leagues

Latt^{de} [122]
₽ D D ~~day ye 16th s~~
57^d : 51^m

Tuesday ye 16th small gales from ye S^o E^t to S W at 2
aftern^n. sounded had 65 fathom at 4 62 fath^m. *112 :4^d: 37^m*
at 63 fath^m at 4 morn^g. had 75 fath^m. some
shattered Ice from ye 16th noon to ye 17th ~~noon~~ ditto
my course made good is S^o 22^d : 30^m W^t. diff Latt^{de}

1 This figure is not clear.

Latt^{de} 29^{m} : 5° Depart^{r}. 11^{m} : 8° dist 32 miles Diggs bears N *~~20 4^{d} 52^{m}~~*
℘DD 19^{d} : 53^{m} E^{t} dist 114 Leagues *20 4^{d} 52^{m}*

57^{d} : 42^{m} Wednesday augst ye 17th fine gales from S^{o} to S E
till midnight it began to blow & rain at 7 Even^{g} made
fast fog at noon saw a seel on ye ice sent a boat
wth 3 hands but could not get him from ye 17th noon
to ye 18th ditto my course made good is S^{o} 43^{d} W^{t} diff
Latt^{de} Latt^{de} 8^{m} : 9° Dep^{tr}. 8^{m} : 3° dist 12 miles diggs bears *W^{t} miles Long*
℘DD N° 20^{d} : 50^{m} E^{t} dist 118 Leagues

57^{d} : 32^{m} Thursday ye 18th small gales from S^{o} E to *124: 4^{d}: 59^{m}*
N^{o} E at 4 afternoon raind at 8 Even made ~~y^{e}~~
fast at 4 morn^{g}. loosed from ye 18th noon to ye 19th ditto
my course made good is S^{o} 19^{d} *.^{m} 50^{m} W Diff latt^{de}
℘DD 20^{m} Dep^{tr} 4^{m} : 6° Dist 12 miles digs bears N° 19^{d} 43^{m}
observ 57^{d} : 18^{m} E^{t} Dist 120 Leagues *varia*

friday ye 19th Easy winds between ye W^{t} & ye N^{o} at 8 Even^{g} *28^{d} : 07^{m}*
sounded had 97 fath^{m}. at 7 morn^{g}. made fast at 10 *125 5^{d} : 01^{m}*
sounded had 87 fath^{m}. all oose had ℘ amplitude
Even^{g}. 28^{d} : 7^{m} variation from ye 19th noon to ye 20 ditto
my course made good is S^{o} 2^{d} : 37^{m} W diff Latt^{de} 11^{m} : 5°
℘DD Dep.^{tr} 1 Dist 12 miles digs bears N° 19^{d} : 57^{m} E^{t} dist
124 Leagues

56^{d}: 53^{m} Saturday ye 20th fog fallin[1] at 2 aftern^{n}. Loosed at *1301*
4 made fast at 8 Loosed wind between ye N & ye E at
one morn^{g} made fast at four loosed ye ice a little
open from ye 20th noon to ye 21st ditto my course made
is S^{o} 15^{d} : 15^{m} west diff Latt^{de} 25^{m} : 4° Dep^{tr}. 5^{m} : 1° Dist
℘ observ 26 *vari*
55^{d} : 36^{m} miles Digs bears N° 19^{d} : 57^{m} E^{t} dist 134 Leagues *26 : 00* *95 : 4^{d} :07^{m}*

Sunday ye 21st fine gales at N^{o} b E Clear at
2 aftern^{n} gott out of ice
at 10 night had 36 fath^{m} at 12: 28 at 2 morn^{g} 22 at 4: 18
fath^{m}. at 6 16 fath^{m} at 8: 22 fath^{m}. at 10: 13 at 12: 13
fath^{m}. Saw ye land bearing S^{o} W B W dist 7 leagues from
ye 21st noon to ye 22^{d} ditto my course made good is S^{o} 25^{d}
17^{m} E^{t} diff latt^{de} 77^{m} : 5° dep^{tr} 35^{m} : 9° Dist 83 miles digs
Latt^{de} ℘ observ bears N° 12^{d} : 30^{m} E^{t} dist 154 leagues *W^{t} Long vari*
54^{d} : 30^{m} [123] *miles* *22^{d} : 30^{m}*

Munday ye 22^{d} fine gales from N^{o} to S W W^{t}erly
from 12 to 2 had from 11 to 18 fath^{m}. from 2 to 4
had 18 & 2 from 4 to 6 had 22 from 6 to 2 morn^{g}.
had ye same from 2 to 4 had 30 fath^{m}. from 4 to 6 *68 : 3^{d} : 17^{m}*
had 34 from 6 to 8 had 33 from 8 to ten had 30 from
10 to 12 had 25 fath^{m}. ye Body of ye bears Islands
bore N^{o} N E dist 6 Leagues from ye 22^{d} noon to y^{e}
23 ditto had my course made good is S^{o} 22^{d} : 30^{m} E^{t}
diff Latt^{de} 64^{m} : 7° Dep^{tr}. 26^{m} : 8° dist 70 miles digs
℘ observ Bears N° 7^{d} : 30^{m} E^{t} dist 174 Leagues

---

1 Ink blot here.

Tuesday ye 23^{d} moderate gales from S^{o} to N^{o}W^{t}erly
53^{d} : 31^{m} from 12 to 2 had from 14 to 10 fath^{m}. from 2 to 4 had
25 fath^{m} from 4 to 6 had 22 & 14 from 6 to 8 had 22
& 23 from 8 to ten had 23 & 21 from 10 to 12 had 19 &
18 from 12 to 2 had 22 & 25 from 2 to 4 had 25 & 23
from 4 to 6 had 20 from 6 to 8 had 20 & 15 from 8 *68 : 3^{d} : 17^{m}*
to 10 had 14 & 11 from 10 to 12 had 10 fath^{m}. a 3
aftern^{n}. took ye perry in a tow at 6 Broke their
tow line at 8 this morn^{g}. took her in a tow wth our
tow line from the 23 noon to ye 24th ditto my course
made good is S^{o} diff latt^{de} 57^{m} dep^{tr} o digs bears
N° 7^{d} : 00^{m} E^{t} dist 194 leagues bears Islands bears
N°8^{D} : 22^{m} E^{t} dist 25 Leagues

[124]

1701

Albany fort Sep^{tr} ye 5th 1701

Honble.
S^{rs}.

I return you humble thanks for ye Lett^{r} you sent me subscrib'd ye 28 of may & having this oppertunity send this to acquaint you y^{t} ye Govr has used all means y^{t} may be to encourage ye ottaways & oth^{r}. Indians to come down & has caused me to make speeches to y^{m} all y^{t} here would come brandy & oth^{r} goods plenty this against their coming & do not doubt but here may be a good trade next year if ye french setting at severn this sumer does not hinder it ye Govr also has sent to ye E^{t} main this sum^{mr} but great part of ye Indians were gone before we came by reason ye breaking up of ye river hove our ship on ye bank of bayleys Iland so y^{t} great part of ye summ^{r}. was spent in getting her of & now is sending me to ye E^{t}main master of ye ship & factory wch trust I shall discharge to ye utmost of my Endeav^{rs}. to increase ye trade of small furs ~~or~~ or any oth^{r} Commoditie y^{t} may ad to your interest & Likewise to ye saving of w^{t} provison I can Honble. Sirs I was desirous to winter at Slude river but ye Govr & council did not think it fitting by reason none is aquainted wth ye breaking up so it is defer'd till next year by wch time I shall be able to give your Hon^{rs}. a bett^{r}. acco^{t}. & hope you will be please to consider my supplying of 2 mens place to ad ten pound to my sala^{r}y as a gratitude if I do well & do believe ye want of a Continual settlement is ye loss of y^{t} trade

[125]

1683-1722

Memorandum of my abode in hudsons bay from 1683 to
1722

In 83 I went out in ye ship lucy Jno. outlaw command^{r}
In 88 after 3 indians being employ'd for great rewards to carry letters from hays river to new severn they return'd wthout performing ye business altho paid then I was sent wth an indian boy & in a month return'd wth answers

In 89 Capt. James young put me & ye same Indian boy ashore to ye N^{o}ward of Churchill river in order to bring to a commerce ye N^{o}thern indians but we saw none altho we travell'd above 200 miles in search of y^{m} & when we came back to churchill ye house was burnt y^{t} was building for y^{t} trade

In 90 ye Comp^{y}. employed 2 french men viz Gooseberry & ~~Gramm~~ Grammair ye former at 80£ ℘ ann^{m}. ye latter at 40 to go amongst ye natives to draw y^{m} to a trade but they did not go 200 miles from ye factory upon wch I was sent away w^{t} ye stone Indians in whose Country I remaind 2 years Enduring much hardships & did increase ye trade considerably as may be perceiv'd by their acco^{t}. books & I return'd to ye factory in 92

In 92 I came to England

In 94 I went again & was taken by ye french & brought home

In 96 was at ye retaking ye fort again

In 97 was taken again when ye hampshire was lost

In 98 went for albany fort wth cap^{t} James knight

In 1701 I was ordain'd master of ye knight frig^{te}. & chief at ye Eastmain formerly ye master of a vessel had 40£ ℘ ann^{m}. & ye trader 40 d^{o}. all wch I dischar'd for 50£ ℘ ann^{m}.

In 1703 I return'd for Eng^{d}.

In 1706 I went out mate of ye perry frig^{te} Jo^{s}. davis Com^{dr} in ord [1] upon my arrival to be chief trader at albany fort or Elsewhere however I was kept out of my Imploy a year by Govr Beal who ye following summ^{r}. sent me in y^{e} ~~Perry~~ knight frig^{te} to ye E^{t} main to gath^{r}. y^{t} trade wch I did

In 1708 I receiv'd ℘ Capt ffullartun y^{r} commission to be deputy under him & he sent me Chief to ye E^{t} main ye same fall & when we returnd ye next spring found by he they had been assaulted by ye french

In 1711 Capt Jno fullartun gave me a Commission bearing date ye 31st July & ye 21st Sep^{tr}. following ye indians brough me word they saw a ship to ye N^{o}ward of ye river I sent boats out to look but did not see ye ship till ye 25th in ye aftern^{n}. ye 26 sent 10 men in ye sloop

1 Edge of paper frayed.

well arm'd likewise 2 indians & their Cannoe on board to be sent on board ye strange ship when ye sloop gott wth out ye sands into 3 fath^{m}. water I also sent 2 indians in anoth^{r}. Cannoe who gott on board as soon as appear'd by Govr Beals coming to

[126]

ye fort in a cannoe I sent in ye sloop who told me it was ye Perry frig^{te}. who in coming into ye river run a ground & ye sloop laid her on board & loaded wth goods to lighter ye perry ye 27th ye sloop came to ye fort & Capt. Beale read his commission & I gave him possession of ye fort ye 29th Capt ward & some of his men came wth ye ill news of ye perrys being bilg'd & sunk so ye sloop went down to her ye same Even^{g}. the 30th this morn^{g}. Govr Beale Desired me to take charge of ye knight to go down to ye Perry to save what could be of ye Cargo accordingly I did & we met ye sloop against ye lower end of Bayleys Isleand ye river being ~~frose~~ full of ice they were forcd to anchor & we gott ye knight aboard ye Perry
Octo^{br} ye 2^{d} we gott ye sloop & knight both to ye fort & took out both their loadings

In 1712 I came to England

In 1714 I went out in ye union Capt. B Harle Comm^{r} wth your commission to be deputy 4 years under ~~him~~ Capt James ~~young~~ knight wth ye benefit of a serv^{t} & if your hon^{rs}. please to peruse those Journals you will find Exerted my utmost to gett a new fort & when you ordered me gov^{r} 1718 I had gott my things on board ye Prosperous hoy in order to winter at churchill to Endeav^{r}. bringing ye nothern trade but this was hindred by ~~reason~~ ^{misfortune} ye hudsonsbay loosing her gripe [1]

In 1719 June 22^{d} the trade being ov^{r} I sailed wth ye prosp^{rs}. for churchill ariv'd ye 30th ye 2^{d} July I sailed w^{t} ye success in comp^{ny}. Jno Handcock master ye 5th traded ~~two of your slaves for 2 Eskemoes~~ wth Eskemoes ye 20th I changed two of your slaves for 2 Eskemoes in order to gett interpeters of their Language & to know w^{t} their Cuntry afforded so I proceeded to ye N^{o}ward seeing & trading wth several parcels of Eskemoes till ye 28th then I return'd & ye 9th of augst. gott to york fort

1719 Augst. ye 24th ye hudsons bay frigg^{te}. was lost where I had a narrow escape for my life & If I had not staid till ye 2^{d} of Sep^{tr}. to get ye cargo ~~out~~ on shore their would have been little of it sav'd but as I did little of it was lost except ye provisions wch was hard upon me having all ye ships comp^{y}. & passengers be

1 This reading is not certain.

[127]

sides those I had before to maintain ye 18th fitted ye [1]
Prosps. hoy for England & all I put on board was not[2]
seven tuns weight & but 34 men & their provission
altho they said I loaded her deep & they return'd ye
next day after they went out being ye 21st & ye 22d wth a
great deal to do I sent her wth 25 men to churchill
ye 7th of march had nine men came from churchill
by my orders for to Ease yt place of provissions

1720 July ye 2d Mr handcock saild wth ye success for churchill
& their to shift into ye Prosps. & to proceed on discovery to
ye Noward having ye 2 Eskemoes wth him to deliver to
their friends & to bring your 2 slaves back but they
was dead 22d July the success arriv'd from Churchill ye
23d sent Mr Lucas in ye success to ye H Bay for goods
ye 27th ye Succs. came here ye 28th I sent her again for goods
& both times gave orders if Capt. ward wanted her to have
ye hudsons bay down to make use of her but not to run
any risque of Loosing her agust ye 1st ye success came
here ye 2d sent her again for ^all ye heavy goods ye 6 ye success came
here ye 9th ye prosps. came her from her nothern discovery
& Mr handcock told me ye albany sloop had winter'd
where he had been last year but he could not
reach yt place ye 10th sent ye success to Churchill to
wait ye arrival of a ship till ye 20th ye prosps. saild
to ye H bay to bring all things of value ye 13th ye pross.
came here withall things except ye bricks & can[3]
balls ye 14th sent ye prosps. for ye rest of ye things ye 21st ye
Prosps. came here from ye standing rigging & all
moveables ye 22d ye succs. came from Churchill ye
26t gave capt ward an ordr. to commd. ye Prosps. &
gett ready to sail by ye last of this month Septr.
ye 1st ye prosps. saild for Engl. ye 2d saw two sail in
the offin ye 3d ye hannah & prosps. anchord against
ye fort ye 7th ye prosps. saild for churchill wth those
goods consign'd to yt place ye 13th I Pilloted ye hannah
to ye lower hole where she continued till ye 18th & then
sail'd for Engl.d ye wind presenting
Septr. ye 25th ye Prosps. return'd from Churchill [4]bran 10 galls.

1721 July ye 26 I saild in ye prosps. wth ye Succs. in compy. James
wapper mastr for churchill ye 30th lost ye success

1 So the copyist. When collated this upper corner of the page had frayed away.
2 Ibid.
3 Edge of paper frayed.
4 Ink of remainder of line is faded.

[128]

July[1] ye 8th took on board ye red & white Earth ye 10th gott to
Churchill[2] the 13th saild for ye Eskemoes cuntry having
Rich^{d}. No^{o}rton & an N^{o}thern indian on board to show
me ye copper ye 21st saw Eskemoes ye 23^{d} saw more Augst. y^{e}
[3]1st saw more ye 9th I bore away because ye winds did not
favour my Intentions of going farther to ye N^{o}ward
to look for ye place where ye albany sloop was lost
we seeing things belonging to those vessels ye 16th I
gott to churchill where we lay wind bound till
ye 28th & I had promised Mr Staunton I would come
back & winter in order to look for y^{e} Copp^{r}. to keep
y^{e} N^{o}thern indians till I return'd to give y^{m} orders
Septr. y^{e} 1st I saw a sloop wch prov'd to be y^{e} whalebone
Jno Senog Mast^{r}. arriv'd from England & Capt
Gofton on board so I went on board to hear w^{t} news
& we rid a very hard ~~strong gale~~ $^{storm\ \&\ they}$ had never an
anchor to trust to but y^{t} on y^{e} ground & he would
have me taken charge of his vessel but I
understood you had ordered me y^{e} contrary
however I told him if he would turn her adrift
I would Endeav^{r}. to save our lives & ship & goods[4]
wth much ado he slipt y^{e} cable wth a buoy as did
also ye prosp^{rs} & thank god we gott both very
well in ye 10th gave all ye 3 Cap^{ts}. their sailing
orders ye 12th all saild & Gofton had a Clause in
his orders to touch at Churchill to take in M^{r}.
Staunton if he could do it by ye 16th

1722 august ye 7th ye mary arriv'd & run aground
on ye cross bar sand & Capt. maclish came
ashore ye 16th ye hannah & whalebone came
in here from Churchill——————

1 So the copyist. When collated the edge here had frayed away.
2 Ibid.
3 Edge of paper frayed.
4 Ibid.

INDEX

Aberdeen, Kelsey refers to, 21
Account of Six Years' Residence in Hudson's Bay, reference to, xxvii
Account of the Countries adjoining to Hudson's Bay, reference to, xxvii
Albany, the wreck of discovered at Marble Island, xxxii
Albemarle, the, sent to Churchill River, 20; collides, 24; men sent to assistance of, 29; supplied with anchor, 63; reference to, 30, 65, 66; hauled ashore to dry at low water, 69
Albourough, men-of-war at, 21
Anne, Queen, Commission of, to Kelsey and Knight, xxxviii
Arrabeck, or Indian language of Hudson's Bay, passage written in, 41
Assinae Poets, Kelsey sent to country of, xxxiii
Assinebouels, the, at Michinipi, xliii; residence of, xliii
Assinebouels of the Meadows, nation of, xliii

Bayley, Captain, reference to xxxix; 21
Bayley's Island, reference to, 78, 80
Beale, Anthony, reference to Journal of, xxxvii; mentioned 79, 80
Bean, Richard, party sent to rescue him, 43
Bear, silver haired, found by Kelsey, 8
Beaver, number of, xxxv; found near Deering's Point, 2; abundance of, 9; brought by Indians to Fort, 30; hands employed in packing skins, 69; trade of, 64
Beaver, Richard, died from broken ribs, 44
Beer, six barrels of, buried, 30; two barrels of, dug up and given to Indians at feast, 52
Belcher, Capt. James, of the *Mary*, xl
Bell, Dr. C.N., paper by, on Henry Kelsey: conclusions of, regarding Lakes Cariboux and Pachegoia, xlv n. 63
Bennet, money paid to, 28
Bishop, Mr. Deputy Governor, reference to, xxxvii; returns to Fort on account of bad weather, 56; returns from hunt having killed one goose, 56; with six hands sets out goose hunting,70; mention of, 71, 72
Black Boy, mention of, 42
Boats, carpenters set to work on, 58; launched in river, 60
Bonaventure, the, takes the *Knight* in tow, 22; runs aground, 22
Bourbon River, reference to, xliii
Bowatter, loses thumb, 29
Brandy, mention of, 28
British Parliamentary Committee of 1749, reference to, xxviii
Buffalo, found in vicinity of Deering's Point, xli; first mention of, by Kelsey, xli; killed by Kelsey, 2, 17; great store of, seen by Indians, 8; method of capture by the Indians, 8; description of, by Kelsey, 17
Buffalo River, mention of, 17
Bull, Edward, assists Kelsey, 19
Bullears, Thomas, son of, found dead, 70
Butlaw, John, disbursements of, for Henry Kelsey, xxxvi

California, the, voyage of, xxix
Canadian Historical Association, paper on Henry Kelsey presented at meeting of, xlv n. 63
Canards Head, mention of, 21
Canoes, large number of, at Fort, 61, 62
Cariboux Lake, reference to, by La France, xliii
Carnaway Water, mention of, 28
Carpenters Tools, discovered in long boat supposed to belong to the *Deering*, 59
Carrot River, reference to, xlv n. 63
Castle Dobbs, Carrickfergus, Dobbs papers in library at, xxix
Caston, mention of, 22
Cedar Lake, claimed to be site of Deering's Point, xlv n. 63
Charcoal, supply of, obtained from Ten Shilling Creek, 68
Cherries, small species found at Deering's Point, 2
Christinaux, country of the, xliii
Churchill, ill-fated journey to, xxxi
Churchill Fort, destroyed by fire, xxxiii
Churchill Journal, the, 1689, xxvii; reveals story of hardships, xxxii
Churchill River, instructions of the HBC regarding, xxxix; Kelsey decides to return to, on account of reluctance of his companion, 17; mention of, 19
Clark, money paid to, 28; mention of, 72
Commentary on the Case of the Hudson's Bay Company, reference to, xxvii
Conn, Hugh, his opinion of site of Deering's Point, xlv n. 63
Cook Room, alterations in, 57, 66
Copper, HBC interested in the discovery of, xxxix; search for, 82
Crimmington, Captain, in command of the *Deering* Frigate, 72
Cross, set up by Kelsey at Deering's Point, 3

Deer Flesh, trade in, 64
Deering, the, reference to, xxiv, xxxiv; takes the *Knight* in tow, 23; mention of, 21, 22; loses her foretopmast, 24; anchor of,

discovered, 30; pinnace of, sunk at her moorings, 71
Deering, Sir Edward, mention of, xiii; name inscribed on cross by Kelsey, xxxiv
Deering's Point, approximate location of, xxxi, xli; Kelsey takes possession of, 10 July 1690, xli; Henry Kelsey's journey from, xlii; Henry Kelsey at, xlii; difference of opinion as to site of, xlv n. 63; peace made with Indians at, 2
Diberveall, Mr. (D'Iberville), see Iberville.
Dictionary of Indian Tongue prepared by Kelsey and printed by HBC, xxxvii
Discovery, the, wrecked at Marble Island, xxxi
Dix, money paid to, 28
Dobbs, Major Arthur F., of Castle Dobbs, xxvii; papers collected by, xxii, xxvii; reference to his writings, xxvii; interested in the discovery of a North-West Passage, xxix; makes no mention of Kelsey before Parliamentary Committee, xxx; note on his narrative of La France, xliii
Dobbs Collection, in Public Record Office, Northern Ireland, xxii, xxvii
Dobbs-Galley, the, voyage of, xxix
Dogside Nation, the, Kelsey seeks to trade with Indians of, 15
Douglas, R., Secretary, Geographic Board, estimate of distance from Carrot River to Cedar Lake, xlv n. 63
Drage, William, clerk of the *California*, published work of, xxix
Draper, Chief Justice, evidence of, xliv n. 42
Ducks, brought into fort, 57
Dutton, Thomas, injury to, 46

Eagles brich, tribe of Indians of that name, ix, 6
East Main, Kelsey trades to, xxxiv; Kelsey chief at, in 1701, x, 79
Ellis, Henry, governor of Georgia, and author of "A Voyage to Hudson's Bay," reference to, xxix, xliii n. 6
Epinette River, reference to, xliii
Eskimoes, Kelsey exchanges two slave boys for two Eskimoes, 80

Firewood, men kept busy in cutting, 31; parties engaged in cutting, for the following winter, 50
Flag of Truce, French send Mohawk demanding surrender of fort, 27; two Frenchmen demand return of prisoners, 72
Flour, supply of, for hunters, 58
Fort Albany, Journal of, xxxvii, xliv n. 36
Fort Churchill, destroyed by fire, xxxiii
Fort Nelson, Kelsey's account of, xxxviii
Fort Prince of Wales, built by Robson, xxx
Fortification, begun on south side of Governor's house, 60
Fourteens, the, men return from, with two Mohawks, 34; partridges brought in from, 34
Foxes, presented to Governor, 65
French, party of Indians sent out to discover if French in vicinity of Hayes River, 25; in vicinity of Hayes River alarm fort, 26; light large fires near English fort, 27; to number of nine hundred besiege fort, 73; demand surrender of fort, 72
French Captain, arrives at fort, 37; his son and his wife leave the factory but return on account of severity of weather, 49; family of, turned out of fort by Governor, 51; at Port Nelson, 70
French Creek, fishing at, 35; hunting at, 36; camped at, 70
French flag, reference to, xxxviii
French Privateers, chase New England brigantine, 21
French Ships, report of, 71; fire on fort, 72
Friendly Society, the, mention of, 73
Fullerton, Governor, leaves Kelsey in charge of fort, xxxviii; appoints Kelsey master of the *Knight*, xxxvii, 79
Fur Trade, effect of British and French traders from Canada on business of Hudson's Bay Company, xlii

Gaston, Captain, mention of, xl
Geese, Kelsey receives supply of, from Indians, 25, traded by Indians for oatmeal, 55; traded by Indians for powder and shot, 59; active trade in, 60
Geyer, Governor of York Fort, xxviii; harsh treatment ascribed to him by tradition, disproved, xxviii; proof that he complied with instructions of HBC furnished by Kelsey Papers, xxviii; instructed to send "Boy Henry Kelsey" to Churchill River, xxix; vindicated by Kelsey Papers, xxxiv; asserts that he has sent Kelsey to the Country of the Assinae poets, xxxvi
Gofton, Capt., ordered to touch at Churchill; reference to, 82
Gooseberry (Groseilliers), and Grammair sent to trade with Natives, xxxiii; reference to, by Kelsey, 79
Gooseberry's House, river frozen over at, 32
Grammair (Grimard), reference to, xxxiii, 79
Grass, with ear like English oats discovered by Kelsey, 3
Great Fork, the, La France at, xliii
Grimard, Elie, xliv n. 23; assists Kelsey, 19. See Grammair.
Grimmington, Captain, mention of, 29. See Crimmington.

Groseilliers, Jean Baptiste, xliv n. 23. See Gooseberry.
Groseilliers, Mèdard Chouart des, xliv n. 23
Guyers Child, mention of, 29; leaves factory, 54

Hampshire, famous actions between the, and the *Pelican*, xxxiv
Handcock, Jno., reference to, 80
Hannah, the, Company resolves not to send ship to the Bay, xl; Kelsey asks for command of, xl; movements of, 81
Hardy, Daniel, death of, 35
Harle, Captain B., reference to, 80
Harrington, Edward, said to have broken ribs of Richard Beaver, 44; death of, 36
Harris, Thomas, 19
Hart, Thomas, said to have engaged in private trade, 20
Hayes River, instructions from Governor of, 15; Kelsey sails for, 19; Kelsey's account of winter at, in 1694, 24; Kelsey's service in carrying letter from Hayes to Severn, 79
Hendry, journey to the Saskatchewan in 1754, referred to, xlv n. 63
Histoirie de l'Amérique Septentrionale, 1722, reference to, xlv n. 55
Home Indians, reference to, ix
Hopewell, the, voyages of Kelsey in, to Indians north of Churchill, 15
Howard, William, badly frozen, 43
Hubbud, Isaac, assists Kelsey, 19
Hubbud, James, gift of book to Henry Kelsey, xxvii, 1
Hudson's Bay Company, ships of, engaged in action against French, xxxiv
Hudson's Bay Company, defence set up by, xxix; charged with failure to discover the North-West Passage, xxix; documents relating to Kelsey in Archives of, xxxii; rights taken by Crown in 1713 for benefit of HBC, xxxviii; Committee acquaint Kelsey with nature of charges made against him, xxxviii; allow Kelsey the whole of proceeds of sale of his furs, xl
Hudson's Bay Frigate, mention of, xix, xxxiv; sails from Hayes River, 37; loss of, 80
Hunters, party sent in search of, 33

Iberville, Sieur d', surrender of York Fort to, xxxi; activities of, xxxiv; reference to, 23; the Governor and fourteen others pass the night in his house, 28; obtains surrender of fort, 73
Ice Chizzels, Indians sent to bring them from the Fourteens, 37
Indians, like White Flag of France better than Union Flag, xxxviii; spend much time in feasting, 7; dead body of Indian burned with ceremony, 7; determined on war, 10; superstitions of, described by Kelsey, xxxi, 11; curious customs of, xvii, 12; in sickness, 12; claim a knowledge of the world beyond, 13; their customs at feasts, 14; report that forty Frenchmen in vicinity of Hayes River, 26; inform Kelsey that French bringing up mortar, 26; distribution of Indian shoes, 31; set out beaver hunting, 35; starving condition of, 35; supplies given to, for starving family, 36; in starving condition seek relief at fort, 39; make snow shoes, 43; with ten days provisions set out to look for deer, 44; come to factory to trade furs, 49; in starving condition come to fort, 55; six canoes come to trade at fort, 59; large number of, come to trade at fort, 61; active trading, 62; arrive at fort from the plains, 65; girl arrives at fort, 68; woman in starving condition given quart of oatmeal, 68
Interpreters, Eskimos used as, 80

Jack, number of, brought in from French Creek, 35
Jack and Tom, the Mohawks, set nets for fish, 67
Johnson, Andrew, deprived of his beaver skins by the Governor, 41
Journal of a Voyage and Journey undertaken by Henry Kelsey, 1691, reference to, xiv, xxix; variations in text of, xxx
Journal of a Voyage in the Deering Frigate from England to Hudson's Bay, in 1698, 73
Journal of Wintering at Hayes River, in 1696, 29

Kelsey, Elizabeth, widow of Henry Kelsey, xl
Kelsey, Henry, activities of, revealed by Kelsey Papers, ix, xxix; Journal of a Voyage and journey undertaken by, xiv, xviii, xxix; problems relating to, xxxii; carries letters from Hayes River to Severn, xxxii; sent to Country of Assinae Poets, xxxiii; brings down a "fleet of Indians," xxxiii; warns Indians that Company will not trade with them unless they cease warfare, xxxiv; becomes Governor of York Fort, xxxiv; makes notes in Indian dialect, xxxv, 41; bravery of, xxxv; salary of, xxxvi; enters service of Company, April 14, 1684, xxxv; salary of, increased, xxxvi; to be rewarded by Guyer, xxxvi; carries gun for fort, xxxvi; appointed chief trader with salary of Deputy Governor, xxxvii; sails to East Main in command of the *Knight*, xxxvii; proposes to serve as Deputy Governor at Port Nelson under James Knight, xxxvii; sails for England with Captain Ward,

xxxvii; to act under direction of Governor at Hudson's Bay, xxxvii; to educate men in literature, xxxvii; left in charge of fort by Governor Fullerton, xxxviii; delayed in England for several months, xxxviii; rewarded by Company, xxxviii; charges made against, xxxviii; considers charges due to malice, xxxix; in letter to Staunton hopes to clear himself of charges, xxxix; obtains supply of whalebone, oil and sea horse teeth, xxxix; his interest in discovery, xxxix; ordered to return home, xxxix; recalled as Governor of York Fort, xl; welcomed by Committee on his return to England, xl; asks for command of the ship *Hannah*, xl; services of, xl; death of, between February 1724, and January 1730, ix, xl; his route in 1691, xli; wanderings of, xli; at Deering's Point, July 10, 1690; leaves York Fort June 12, 1690, xiii, xli; comment on, xli; returns to England in Hudson's Bay ship, xlii; describes in rhyme the hardships he endured in the year 1690, 1; names neck of land Deering's Point, 2; his determination to acquire a knowledge of Native language, 1; leaves Deering's Point to see Stone Indians, 3; pitches tent in woods, 4; scarcity of food on journey, 5; addresses the Indians requesting them to wait for his party, 5; Indians present him with 17 beaver skins, 6; invited to a feast by the Indians, 8; invited to join war party of Indians, 8; meets Indians and delivers his message to them, 9; discourages Indians from going to war, 9; informs Indians that Governor will not trade with them if they go to war, 10; urges Stone Indians to make peace, 10; makes presents to the Indians, 11; swims across river as raft would not carry weight, 18; takes great risks in shooting rapids, 18; expresses desire to go to England, 19; declines to take part in any voyage of discovery until he receives orders from England, 19; claims he is unable to keep journal, 20; receives supply of powder and shot from Governor, 25; goes up river in search of fish, 30; set out with Mr. Newton for Port Nelson but returned on account of bad weather, 37; gives reason for writing passage in Indian language, 41; perilous journey of, for plank, 42; token sent to him given to another person by the Indian named Whiskers, 47; remains in marsh for Governor's signal, 58; returns from the marsh, 59; journal of, in 1698, 73; asks for increase of salary, 78; memorandum by, 79; saves ship's cargo, 80; sails for Eskimos country, 82
Kelsey, John, interest of the Company in, xl
Kelsey, William, reference to, xliv n. 53
Kelsey Papers, destroy myth current for 200 years, xxviii; prove accuracy of Company's statements regarding Kelsey, xxviii; value of, in determining historic truth, xxviii
Keneday, George, petition of, xl
Kenney, Dr. James F., Kelsey papers transcribed under supervision of, xxvii
Knight, the, reference to, xxiv, 22, 23, 29, 80
Knight, Captain James, sufferings of, xxxi ; discovered by Esquimaux, xxxi; unfortunate voyage of, xxxi; disastrous voyage of, xxxviii; reference to, xi, xxv, 80
Knight, Governor, recommendation of Kelsey by, xxxvi
Knox, William, Governor of Nova Scotia, reference to, xxix

La France, Joseph, quoted by Dobbs, xliii
La Potherie, quoted by Dobbs, xlii
La Potherie and Jeremie, reference to, xlii
Lastaf, man-of-war at, 21
La Vérendrye, lead plates of, on banks of Missouri, xlv n. 63
Leveson-Gower, Mr., reference to, xxxii
Lucy, the, John Outlaw, Commander, xxxii

MacLish, Thomas, appointed to succeed Kelsey as Governor of York Fort, xl; reference to, 82
Martin, (Marten), the first caught during winter, 32; presented to Governor by Indians, 65
Mary, the, Kelsey to return in, xl; runs aground, 82
Matthew, Mr., sent with flag of truce to the French with terms of surrender, 28
Medicine Men, Kelsey's reference to, xxxv
Memorandum by Kelsey of his residence in Hudson's Bay, from 1683, 79
Michinipi, or *Great Water*, description of, xlii; probably Lake Winnipeg, xliii
Miss-Top-Ashish, name applied to Kelsey, xxx
Mohawks, kill partridges at Ten Shilling Creek, 46
Moor, money paid to, 28
Moose, brought in by Indians, 5
Moose Lake Route, reference to, xlv n. 63
Mortar, set up at end of Governor's house, 51
Mountain Poets, reference to, ix; Kelsey sends party in search of, 7

Nawatamee Chief, powwow with, xlii
Nayhathaway Indians, three killed by Naywatamee Poets, xxxiv; reference to, ix,

xlii; Indians with Kelsey afraid of, 6; fail to keep the peace, 11.
Naywatamee Poets, reference to, ix, xxix; promise to come to trade at Bay, xxxiv; Kelsey's search for the, xl; journey undertaken to promote trade with, in 1691, 3; kill three women of the Nayhathaways, 6; Kelsey desires to meet them, 7
Nelson River, source of, xlii; reference to, by La France, xliii; and Hayes River routes referred to, xliii
New England Brigantine chased by French privateers, 21
Newton, Mr., disagrees with the Governor and is turned out of his house, 40: Governor takes the keys of the fort from him, 47; returns to fort with ten geese, 57; wounded by shot when returning to fort dies of wounds, 72
North-West Passage, voyages for the discovery of, undertaken by public subscription, xxix
Norton, Richard, to assist Kelsey in search of copper, 82

Oars, carpenters employed making, 58
Ottaways, the, mention of, 78
Ounipique Lake, described by La France, xliii

Palisades, set up round the Governor's house, 30; removed from Governor's house, 60
Partridges, brought in by hunters, 34
Paul, money paid to, 28
Pelican, famous action between *Hampshire* and the, xxxiv
Perry Frigate, Kelsey mate of, xxxv; cargo of, salvaged by Kelsey, xxxv; mention of, 73; cargo of saved by Kelsey, 80; reference to, xxiv, 80
Pipe, its construction and use, 12
Pitts, money paid to, 28
Poets, suffix attached to the name of several Indian tribes, xliii n. 9
Poplo Wood found at Deering's Point, xli
Port Nelson, traders at, xlii; Kelsey anchors at, 19; two ships arrive at, 26; Indians at, 29; Indians on south side of, 56; geese seen at, 56; Stone Indians from, arrive at fort, 63
Pratt, Edward, assists Kelsey, 19; money paid to, 28
Prosperous, the, Kelsey takes command during a gale, xxxv; reference to, 81

Rabbits, number of, 39; eight traded for five pints of oatmeal, 52
Radisson , voyages of, reference to, xliv n. 9
Raft, construction of to convey goods across river, 18; timber for fort, reference to 64; difficulties of rafting, 70
Rainy Lake, description of, by La France, xliii
Red Earth, shipment of, 82
River De Vieus Hommes, description of, xliii
River of Blood Red Colour, described to Kelsey, 6
River Savanne or Epinette, reference to, xliii
Robson, Joseph, reference to works of, xxvii; statements by, xxviii; reference to, xxx; scathing narrative of, xxx; stone mason, supervisor of buildings of HBC, xxx; his account of Kelsey, xxx; claims that vocabulary of Indian language suppressed by HBC, xxxvii

St. Margarets Hope, reference to, 22
Ste. Theresa (York Fort), reference to, xlii
Sargeant, Governor, instructions to, xxix
Saskatchewan, first visit of white man to, in 1690, xli
Saskatchewan River, reference to, xlv n. 63
Savage, Thomas, to accompany the Boy Henry Kelsey, xxix; accompanies Kelsey, xxxii, xxxiii; gives instructions to Kelsey which he refuses to obey, 19
Savanne River, reference to, xliii
Seaford, the, reference to, 21, 22; pinnace of, runs ashore, 30; repairs to pinnace of, 65; Mr. Bishop and nine hands set out in the pinnace of, to watch movement of strange ships, 72
Senog, John, reference to, 82
Severn, report of a boat near, 67; French at, 79
Shot, manufacture of, 55; hands at fort engaged in melting, 62
Slate Mines observed by Kelsey, xlii; seen by Kelsey, 7
Slaves, exchange of, for boys of the country, xxxix; death of, 127
Slude River, Kelsey anxious to winter at, 78
Smith, Mr., letter of Kelsey to, xix, 20
Smithson, Captain, report of, 72
Smith's Shop, construction of, 57
Smoke used as a signal, 16
Songs, interpretation of by Indians, 13
Spencer, Kitt, kills goose, 55; ordered to the marsh by Governor, 58
Staunton, letter from Kelsey to, regarding charges preferred against himself, xxxviii; reference to, 82
Staysmore, Joseph, causes trouble in the fort, 27
Stone Indians, reference to, ix; on the Saskatchewan, xli; met by Kelsey near Deering's Point, xlii; agree not to molest the Naywatamee Poets, 10; creed of, differs from that of the Nayhathaways, 14; 27 canoes of, at fort, 62

Success, the, reference to, 81
Swans, killed by Indians for food, 5
Sweatah Island, mentioned, 22

Ten Shilling Creek, reference to, 49, 51, 70; Indians at, 44; raft sent from, to fort, 66
Thorpness, departure of Kelsey from, 73
Tobacco, powder and other articles stored by Kelsey for return journey, 4
Trade, loss of, due to want of continual settlement, 78
Trout, numbers of, brought to fort, 32; and other fish caught in river, 60

Umfreville, his reference to Robson as a candid writer, xxx
Union, the, Kelsey sails in, 80
Upland Indians, come to trade furs at fort, 47
Utrecht, Treaty of, position of HBC re-established under, xxxi; reference to, x, xxxiv, xxxvii, xlii

Vickary, Matthew, death of, 34

Ward, Captain, sails with Kelsey for England, xxxvii; reference to, 81
Washa, Captain of Mountain Poets sends message to Kelsey, 8
Waskashreeseebee, place of that name, xlii; Kelsey requested to meet Indians at that place, 5
Wessguaniconan, headdress worn by Indians, 11
Whalebone, the, arrival at Churchill, xxxii; reference to, xxxv, 82
Whales, HBC's interest in, xxxix; report of white, 65
Whiskers, Indian by that name engages in private trade, 41; suffers from lack of food, 47; conveys food to his starving family, 47; turned out of the fort by Governor, 47
Wolves, destroy deer near Port Nelson, 31; in fight with dog on river, 49
Women, indifferent treatment of in sickness, 13
Wood, scarcity of, 16; men engaged in sawing planks, 54
Wooden Bows, used by the Natives near Deering's Point, 2

York Fort, daily life at, xx, xxi; Kelsey's part in recapture acknowledged by Committee of Hudson's Bay, xxxvii
Young, Captain James, in command of the *Hopewell*, 15; sets party ashore, 17; money paid to, 28; reference to, by Kelsey, 79